AWAY WITH WORDS

Young Writers' 16th Annual Poetry Competition

It is feeling and force of imagination that make us eloquent.

How can I not dream while writing? The blank page gives a right to dream.

Young Writers

Eastern England

Edited by Lynsey Hawkins

 Young**Writers**
First published in Great Britain in 2007 by:
Young Writers
Remus House
Coltsfoot Drive
Peterborough
PE2 9JX
Telephone: 01733 890066
Website: www.youngwriters.co.uk

SB ISBN 978-1 84602 821 2

Foreword

This year, the Young Writers' *Away With Words* competition proudly presents a showcase of the best poetic talent selected from thousands of up-and-coming writers nationwide.

Young Writers was established in 1991 to promote the reading and writing of poetry within schools and to the young of today. Our books nurture and inspire confidence in the ability of young writers and provide a snapshot of poems written in schools and at home by budding poets of the future.

The thought, effort, imagination and hard work put into each poem impressed us all and the task of selecting poems was a difficult but nevertheless enjoyable experience.

We hope you are as pleased as we are with the final selection and that you and your family continue to be entertained with *Away With Words Eastern England* for many years to come.

Contents

Alex Chapman (15)   37
Alexander Catley (16)   38
Philip Everitt (15)   39
Amber Golledge (15)   40
Adam Shewan (15)   41
Esther Idowu (15)   42
Louise Rattray (15)   43
Kerrie Longman (15)   44
Hayley Dunn (15)   45
Katie Ward (12)   46
Sean McKean (12)   47
Reece Wilson (12)   48
Kirsty Farrant (15)   49
Charlotte Whiteley (15)   50
Zoe Batchelor (15)   51
Emma Bailey (15)   52
Lewis Mansfield (15)   53
Peter Harrison (15)   54
Max Gammer (15)   55

Bottisham Village College, Cambridge

Shannon Thompson (12)   56
Stephanie Blanco (13)   57
April Spencer (12)   58
Alex Breeze (12)   59
Joe Wilson (12)   60
Chay Appadoo (12)   61
Addam Morley (12)   62
Hayden Fuller (12)   63
Otis Moorman (12)   64
Alex Nicholls (12)   65
Shannon Copare (13)   66
Amanda Dawson (12)   67
Sam Stringer (11)   68
Alice Hubbard (11)   69
Jenny Shelley (11)   70
Sarah Loker (11)   72
Georgia Morris (11)   73
Georgia Hellmers (11)   74
Abi Pain (11)   75

Ferrers Specialist Arts College, Higham Ferrers

Hadleigh High School, Ipswich

Siân Hammond (13)	142
Lucy Mackie (13)	143
Matt Grimwade (13)	144
Ross Bray (13)	145
Ryan Wood (13)	146
Ryan Clemson (13)	147
Zoe Alleyne (13)	148
Adam Higgins (12)	149
Ashley De Banks (13)	150
Yolanda Rankin (13)	151
Michael Rose (13)	152
Rebecca Le Grice (13)	153
Vicky White (13)	154
Ben Hart (14)	155
Melissa Parker (13)	156
Kate Loder (12)	157
Jodie Smart (12)	158
Ayrton Artiss (11)	159
Abigail Slade (12)	160
Frazer Last (11)	161
Harrison Boote (12)	162
Billie Tearney (11)	163
Hannah Maxwell (12)	164
Emma Jackson (12)	165
Gemma Bloomfield (12)	166
Sam Taylor (12)	167
Jacob Ebbs (12)	168
Emily Lewis (12)	169
Ruhel Amin (12)	170
Ella Delves (11)	171
Katie Gant (11)	172
Nicole Ellis-Tattersdale (11)	173
Jade Richards (11)	174
Brett Crisp (11)	175
Kate Tabrett (14)	176
Sara Rea (13)	177
Chris Brown (13)	178
Bethany-Jane Harvey (13)	179
Ryan Farthing (13)	180
James Leeder (13)	181

Sam Mitchell (13)	182
Sophie Benton (14)	183
Sam Hunt (13)	184
Rachel Underhill (13)	185
Shelley Horwood (13)	186
Jess Robeson (14)	187
Carly Bledul (13)	188
Liam Self (11)	189
Jadene Heffer-Thorpe	190
Sophie Green (11)	191
Max Highland (11)	192
Madeleine Sweeting (12)	193
Daniel Leathers (13)	194
Aidan Bignell (13)	195
Harry Evans (12)	196
Elvina Williams (11)	197
Kirsty Fisher (11)	198
Brendon Wardley (11)	199
Alice Partridge (12)	200
Georgia Dashfield (11)	201
Anastasia Wyatt (11)	202
Rebekah Grant (11)	203
Jake Howard (11)	204
Mollie Hart (11)	205
Rebecca Warner (11)	206

The Poems

Fashion

I have a passion
That is fashion
My favourite clothing is my baker boy hat
That's the only thing that doesn't make me look fat
My dream is to be a fashion designer one day
I hope I become one next May
My image is important to me
Being a top fashion designer is what I want to be.

Sarah Earl

Miss Smith

A round multicoloured button
From a smart brown office skirt
Left in McDonalds
Worn by the Prime Minister's secretary
Who liked to go to nightclubs on a Friday night
She dreamed about film stars
And got cross when people were rude to her
She was unselfish and pretty
And thought about other people.

Stacey Allington
Beacon Hill Special School, Ipswich

Tilly Tots

A round garnet coloured button
From a fancy lilac winter dress
Left in a blue and green dance hall
Worn by a ballet dancer
Who liked to go dancing on a Friday night
She dreamed about being famous
And got cross when her dress got covered in mud
She was beautiful and loved to dance
She thought about swans and poodles.

Mica Cox
Beacon Hill Special School, Ipswich

Mr Johnson

A round black button
From a long dark overcoat
Left in KFC
Worn by a head teacher
Who liked to mark his books on a Friday night
He dreamed about getting married
And got cross when children didn't listen to him
He loved his school
And thought about helping children.

Sophie Faulkener
Beacon Hill Special School, Ipswich

Jasmin

A round, pale green, flowery button
From a pretty green summer dress
Left in a cinema
Worn by a pretty, little, blonde-haired girl
Who liked to play with her dolls
And watch TV on a Friday night
She dreamed about meeting a pop star
And got cross when she was told to go to bed early
She wanted a pet
And thought about saving her pocket money for one.

Kirsty Hazelwood (13)
Beacon Hill Special School, Ipswich

Simon Doctor

A round black 4-holed button
From a pair of black trousers
Left in a cinema
Worn by an old man
Who liked to go the cinema on a Friday night
He dreamed about being rich
And got cross when people laughed at him
He got drunk when things went really well
And thought about his friend who died in the war.

Daniel Doctor
Beacon Hill Special School, Ipswich

Captain Taylor

A large round bottle-green button
From a long dirty army coat
Left in a cemetery
Worn by an old army colonel
Who liked to get drunk on a Friday night
He dreamed about Adolf Hitler
And got cross when people talked about the war
He was grumpy and liked to be by himself
He died last year.

Nathan Whatling
Beacon Hill Special School, Ipswich

A Lost Old Lady

A large round button
From a long, dark green raincoat
Left in a KFC
Worn by an old lady
Who liked to meet her friends
And play bingo on a Friday night
She dreamed about winning lots of money
And got cross when they were losing
She had a special pen
And thoughts about winning lots of things.

Christian Outridge
Beacon Hill Special School, Ipswich

The Rock Star

A small black button
From a leather jacket
Left at a gig on Friday night
Worn by a rock star
Who liked to jam on a Friday night
He dreamed about fit girls
And got cross when he woke up the next day
He was a cruel man
And thought about drink and drugs.

Matt Lucas (14)
Beacon Hill Special School, Ipswich

Queen Victoria

A white crystal button
From a pure silk wedding dress
With a long train and body veil
Left in an old dusty wardrobe
Worn by Queen Victoria
Who loved to go to a ball on a Friday night
She dreamed about getting married
And got angry when she found out
He was in love with another woman!
She put a curse on the woman
So that every night she turned into a swan
She thought about destroying the swan
And making her sweetheart fall back in love
With her.

Sarah Edwards (14)
Beacon Hill Special School, Ipswich

Princess

A grand slender button
From a fascinating ballgown
Left in the loft
Worn by Princess Fiona
Who liked to go dancing on a Friday night
She dreamed about dancing with Prince Charming
And got cross when the ball was cancelled
She opened a bottle of champagne, ran a bath,
And thought about the day she would get married and be Queen.

Gavin Wilding (16)
Beacon Hill Special School, Ipswich

Refugees

They come with their boxes
Some are happy
Some are very sad indeed
They wear green coats
They are crowded
Some are even confused
Most of their boxes are tied with string
Some of their boxes have clothes in
They're helping with each other
Soldiers watch with guns.

Robert Goh (14)
Beacon Hill Special School, Ipswich

War Will Kill Us

Do you think war will kill us all?
It could be today or tomorrow
God can't help us!
Nobody can help us!
The big man says He cares
Do you think that?
London is bombed
New York buildings collapse
One big bomb can kill us all
We have no chance!
This is war!

Sean Upson (14)
Beacon Hill Special School, Ipswich

Refugee Camp

The children are scared and alone
They have lost their families
They have lost their friends
They have nowhere to go
Is war worth it?

Vanessa Coleman (14)
Beacon Hill Special School, Ipswich

War

Why did it happen to us?
Mum and her children
Had to leave their country
We had to go to another country
I have a brother
And a sister
Where will we go?

Sarah Handscombe (15)
Beacon Hill Special School, Ipswich

Helicopters

Three helicopters hover
Soldiers are undercover
They watch and talk into walkie talkies
A truck stands by
They feel angry
They are worried
Soldiers in war.

Dan Baltadonis (15)
Beacon Hill Special School, Ipswich

Terrorist Attack

The World Trade Center
In New York is being destroyed
People have died
People are scared
People are crying
It was horrible
Now it's war.

Tom Clements (15)
Beacon Hill Special School, Ipswich

Friends

Our party is over
We have lost our loved ones
Our friends have died
We pray for their souls
We lay flowers in their memory
We will always remember.

Jamie Gooch
Beacon Hill Special School, Ipswich

Exploding Missiles

We got hit and hurt
We are sad
We want to be in peace
But we want to help our land
We are dying!
We want to win the war
For our land.

Matthew Poole (14)
Beacon Hill Special School, Ipswich

Silly Old Granddad

His twinkling old eyes
Not many teeth
Dark black hair
Like coal in a fireplace

Calendars everywhere
His home is so warm
Always biscuits in the tin
Dolphins everywhere like in the sea.

Telling tales of his life
WW2 is so interesting
Talking in Japanese
Walking every day
Like a heard of animals never stopping.

With his East London voice
I hear all the time
His low-pitch voice
Like a lion's roar

Oh how I would miss
My silly old granddad
If he were to move away
Oh I hope he will stay forever.

Holly Adams (12)
Beauchamps High School, Wickford

Nanny Nita

Her twinkling blue eyes
Like the sun shining on the ocean
Her smile makes everybody happy and welcome
When you see her beautiful face.

The new modern house
All clean and fresh inside
The pictures of the family
Right by your side

As you enter her studio
You see the wonderful things she paints
Sunsets and landscapes
Up on the wall

I miss you so dearly
Whenever you go away
God bless you Nanny Nita
I love you in every way.

Hannah Mansfield-Smith (12)
Beauchamps High School, Wickford

Nanny Norris

Twinkling blue eyes
Like a clear blue ocean
Long white hair
Like the beautiful white snow

Staring into space
With a brew in her hand
I sneeze as the smell
Of the musky house reaches my nose

'Bingo!' she shouts
As she wins the jackpot
She wears her blouse
As if it was cool

But if she left my life
I wouldn't know what to do
But I know one thing
That my life wouldn't be the same.

Adam Beeson (12)
Beauchamps High School, Wickford

Nannie Pat

Twinkling blue eyes like a clear river
Soft cheeks, a little wrinkled
Her eyes that go all puppy dog-eyed when I leave
That's my nan.

She walks slowly
But thinks she's going fast
Chatting all the way
That's my nan.

She likes a cup of tea
And a biscuit too
She sits and does her crosswords
That's my nan.

She puts on her tights
And her flowery dress
And her favourite coat
That's my nan for sure.

Jordanne Underwood (12)
Beauchamps High School, Wickford

My Great-Nanny Langley

My great-nan
She's so sweet
She's fantastic
She's so petite

Her eyes are like stars in the sky
The clothes that she wears always catch my eye.

Her movement is slow
But that doesn't matter
Whoever you are
She likes a natter

She wobbles her cheeks
To make me laugh
She knits away
To make a scarf

I'd hate it if she went away
I'd cry all night and day
I'd want her to come back home
So she could make me a lovely hot scone.

Jade Langley (12)
Beauchamps High School, Wickford

Nana

Her twinkling blue eyes
Like the sun on the ocean
The smile that is always there on your face
The white curly hair
That always looks nice
Walking slowly but taking care with every step

The beautiful essences as you walk through the door
The hilarious pictures of the rest of your family
The bread and banana that you always eat
The voice that you hear that never stops talking.

The seat you always sit in
The shoes that you can't take off
The wallpaper you have
That's as colourful as the rainbow
The clothes that I see just in so many colours.

The windows I see covered by china
The mirrors I never see on the walls
The magazines that sit beside your chair
The chair lift that lets you go upstairs

I would never survive if you left me
Please don't go without hearing this poem
Because it tells you lots of things
About your fabulous and beautiful self
And also it shows that I love you in every way.

Hannah Rattray (12)
Beauchamps High School, Wickford

Nanny Eileen

Twinkling green eyes like
Fresh grass in the spring
Her eyes shine as brightly
As the Northern Lights

A warm smile making everyone happy
Teeth as white as pearls
A beautiful face
As happy as the sun

She glides across the floor
Carefully as she walks
Into the kitchen
To make a cup of tea

Her house is lovely
It makes you feel so welcome
With flowers on the wallpaper
And photos everywhere

Her hobbies are gardening
And shopping too
Her garden is full
Of beautiful flowers

She has pretty clothes
And shoes as well
She is never out of fashion
She is so cool

Nanny Eileen if you went away
I would miss you soooo much
You could never tell
How much I'd miss you.

Chloe Tetu (12)
Beauchamps High School, Wickford

My Poem

Her soft curly hair
As shiny as silk
It smells like a fresh bed
Of flowers

She's the happiest person
That I've ever met
When she laughs
Everyone laughs with her

If you meet my nan
You'll know it's her
She has that same gleam in her eyes
That shows she's a caring nanny.

She's always there for me
When I'm not feeling 100 per cent
Even if you're not one of her own,
She would love and care for you.

Because she is my nan, like no other!

Carrie Kirby (12)
Beauchamps High School, Wickford

My Nan

You have twinkling blue eyes like on a summer's day
And are happy like Christmas Day
You are always smiling like a summer's day.

Whenever I go round to see you
I know I will probably get a hot chocolate with some biscuits on a tray
You are always on the move.

Your home always smells nice and is always clean and tidy
Decorated with pictures of friends and family and yourself on holiday
With Granddad
You have loads of medals and trophies that you and Granddad
Have got over the years from bowls and other sports
You also have lots of china ornaments around the fireplace and house.

I can't wait to see you play bowls again
I hope I can help you out on the stalls again
You always have a soft sweet voice
And wear old people's clothes
But don't worry I still love you.

If you ever went away to move house far away,
So I couldn't see you very often,
I would cry all night, especially if you move to another country.
I love you loads and loads.

Daniel Quirke (12)
Beauchamps High School, Wickford

My Granddad

My granddad

Twinkling blue eyes like the vast ocean
Always smiling like the sun
The loving round face
Bringing warmth to the world.

My granddad

Slowly shuffling round and round
With walking stick in his hand
Bent over
But he was still going strong.

My granddad

Beautiful garden
Full of plants and flowers
Lots of books I used to read
Lots of his medals
Tucked away in a drawer.

My granddad.

Emily Beckwith (12)
Beauchamps High School, Wickford

My Nan

Twinkling blue eyes like the stars above
A soft skin like cats' hair
A lovely smile which shows her love
And that one gold tooth

She moves like a strong tiger
She always moves smoothly
She will never fall over
And she stands tall

Her house is very peaceful
It's always been clean
She always has that table
That would not disappear

She always recycles
To help the environment
She used to take me camping
And sometimes take me swimming

I will always love you
Even with Granddad gone
You will be in my heart forever
And that's where you belong.

Matthew Ives (12)
Beauchamps High School, Wickford

Nanny Snoopy

My nanny is the best
Glistening blue eyes like the summer seas
A beautiful face in its own way
Soft, shiny hair like silky sand
Always playing with the dog
Always making a cup of tea
A beautiful flowery home
Always smells of Lenore
Knitting cardigans, sewing dresses, walking the dog, planting flowers
Baggy tops and black trousers
She speaks so softly
If she left I would cry
I love her a billion times around the world.

Codie Moxey (12)
Beauchamps High School, Wickford

Nanny Marion

Eyes that sparkle like the stars
Her soft peach skin that has a little wrinkle
Always smiling like the sun
She bakes cakes for every occasion
Family photos and ornaments in the cabinets,
Walks the dog twice a day,
If I or you ever move I will miss you!

Imogen King (12)
Beauchamps High School, Wickford

What I Love About Nanny Mai

Twinkling eyes like the stars in the night sky
Soft, silky skin and always smiling
Her short shiny hair
Always full of life like a cloud of bubbles.

The modern house
Smelling so fresh
Always clean and tidy
The bed of flowers in the back garden.

Photos of the family
Around the whole place
Always treating us to goodies
Making tea as if it's a race

How I love you so much
To the moon and back
How I would miss you so
Thank you x.

Lauren Wells (13)
Beauchamps High School, Wickford

Hotels And Shacks

I travelled down the motorway towards the airport sign
Driving a rented car, it wasn't mine
The plane was delayed to my destination
I was travelling far out, out of this world into another nation
In the morning when I was departing
My passport, tickets and luggage I would be carting
So I went to the hotel, because delayed
Travelling to a job where I wouldn't be paid
I got a very nice room, the penthouse suite
Then I called room service for something to eat
It came on a plate with the silver cutlery,
My last delicious meal,
I had to forget my gluttony,
So I went to bed, to rest my head
And ponder on the words my father had said
The next thing I knew I awoke from sleeping
From the sound of a taxi's horn beeping
It was time for me to place
For another place where no reason exists
To have a smiley face
Once in the cab I became nervous in every single way
No idea what I'd say
To the children of a dying country
When I landed it was not what I expected
The brightest sun that had ever existed,
A nice day,
In England.
But the sun was the only thing that has never changed,
This constant has over time made the skin crack and become
Orange, like the face of an elderly woman in Spain.
It was plain, to see what I was here to do.
To give them hope of a better life
A clean glass of water, this was something new
I travelled on a dirt road rather than a motorway,
When I arrived at my shack,
I thought, how can I live this way?

When I saw the children,
I had found my motivation to stay,
So if I could choose between hotels and shacks,
Then I would choose shacks,
Although the shack is plain,
What the shack lacks the children gain.

Michael Neaves (15)
Beauchamps High School, Wickford

My Home

They sent me a football shirt
My favourite team
Sky-blue and white
Glowing like gold
Fantastic trophies, shining silver
Football carries on in England
My true home

I miss the players
I miss the goals
I miss the thrill of a win
I miss my home

I dream of my birthplace
From nineties photographs
I long to go back to England
Go back to my home.

Jack Brown (15)
Beauchamps High School, Wickford

Brazilian Birthdays

In the morning at my council estate
I went downstairs for a very important date
My birthday today and I was sent gifts
From Brazil I found the one from Auntie Kiff.

The gift sat all on its own
Like a lonely boy who wants to go home
He opened the present with a fist full of joy
To find for himself his very best toy
His uncle's best pen, oh what a happy boy.

Alex Chapman (15)
Beauchamps High School, Wickford

A Letter From Ashmad

I haven't spoken for five days now
Nothing, that's all I have
I've barely been here for seven days
Moved out of Baghdad alone without my family
They're all gone.

I now sleep in the living room of cousin Rashmad's flat
Aunt says I need to go to school
Walked in on that next Monday not knowing what to do or expect
By lunchtime I was hated because of the war
At lunch I sat on my own watching smiles go by,
I really miss my clothes
And my frown just grew longer.

I got back to my artificial home where I was bundled by my aunt
I looked down and placed in my new hands was a letter
A letter from Ashmad in Baghdad
My eyes shifted from left to right
A smile came across my face as reminders came to me of home.

I now have a smile on my face
Even though I find it hard to fit in
I do wish I could go back as now I am not sure
Am I English or Iraqi?

Alexander Catley (16)
Beauchamps High School, Wickford

Far From The Amazon

The six of us looked down on the world
Far from the wildlife
My lip piercing gave funny looks
Far from the Amazon

The six of us went to live
Deep into the city like a forest of fireflies
Surrounded by technology
Far from the Amazon

The six of us went to school
My uniform like a bite
We spent the day alone
Far from the Amazon

The six of us went to the Thames
Astounded by the boats
Unlike our wooden kayaks
Far from the Amazon

The six of us picked up parcels
Tribal clothes from parents
Reminded us we were . . .

Far from the Amazon!

Philip Everitt (15)
Beauchamps High School, Wickford

India Is Too Far From Home

My nostrils are taken aback by the strong spices
And I awake to the sounds of the chimes above,
Blowing in the wind,
Through the stained glass window I see my grandmother,
Smothered head to toe in every piece in exquisite jewellery imaginable,
The colours glisten like the rare evening sunsets back in England,
Even though blood is shared, I do not see myself in Grandmother,
We are too different,
India is far from home.

I glance at the picture of Mama and Papa beside me,
Oh how I miss them,
How I miss the likeness that we shared,
Unlike Grandmother and I,
As I open my wardrobe the colours beam,
Blinding my delicate, fragile eyes
How do I choose from this array of flamboyant clothes
That are alien to me?
I long for denim and cotton, the things I took for granted back home,
India is too far from home.

My tongue is on fire and I swallow to relieve the pain,
My stomach is rumbling - pleading for me to satisfy its needs
But my taste buds cannot stomach the peculiar food before me
I wish I could eat Mama's home cooked Shepherd's Pie one last time
But India is too far from home.

Amber Golledge (15)
Beauchamps High School, Wickford

An Alien Culture

Arriving at the airport, I didn't feel right
I stick out like a sore thumb
As I'm the only white.

I made my way outside, and felt the burning heat
I flagged down a taxi,
And sat on the back seat.

As I thought of what I left behind, I held back a tear
This country is so strange to me,
I won't fit in here.

I feel so alien wearing these clothes, everyone stares at me
I feel so intimidated by these stares,
That's easy to see.

I hope I can adapt to this new culture and learn to fit in well
But whatever happens will happen
And only time will tell.

Adam Shewan (15)
Beauchamps High School, Wickford

My New Start

My new home
My new country
My new life

My new sea blue cut jeans I got to meet
My new friends at my new school

The new dull grey colour of the new city
The new fear I feel on my first day
The new realisation that I am in a new county
With a new peculiar language, that makes no sense to me.

But then I think of my old life, and the war . . .
How most of my old and familiar friends are dead
How my regular old school and my regular old house were burnt down
Most of all I thought about my beautiful beloved
State was in a state of pending doom

And here I am

My new home
My new country
My new life

I have a chance for a new start
I thank God for that.

Esther Idowu (15)
Beauchamps High School, Wickford

I Stand . . .

I stand, dazed by the colour, the richness
Red and orange fabrics flail through the air
Like flames, roaring in the sky
I watch the Chinese dancers, as two form one
As they show the actions of the lion,
As I see a part of their culture.

I stand, stunned by the detail, the extravagance
The pure animal hair brush, whips across the page,
Like a predator after its prey,
I watch the Chinese painter, as he makes beauty
As he shows meaning,
As I see a part of his culture.

I stand, amazed by the movements, the art
Turning and twisting, jumping and leaping
Like something trapped, trying to break free
I watch the Chinese martial artists, as they fight
As they show complete power and knowledge,
As I see a part of their culture.

Louise Rattray (15)
Beauchamps High School, Wickford

Hindu Wedding

Covered from head to toe in blood-red satin
Beaming like the sun in the sky
Smothered in beautiful golden bangles
Glistening like a jewel in the distance

Watching my sister emerge from the distance,
Bindis, winding, twirling up her hand
Entering on a majestic elephant,
Decorated with deep red purple and embodied to perfection.

Marvelling at the contrast to an English wedding
Replacing snow white dresses for radiant red saris
Feeling like an intruder
Replacing soft fluffy cake for sweet tangy spices.

Kerrie Longman (15)
Beauchamps High School, Wickford

Poem

My family sent me some presents
From my luxury London home
Voi jeans
As blue as the ocean
Lacoste jumpers as colourful as the rainbow

I tried them on
In front of my new room mates
I'm the odd one out
Walking down the street

While they are in their rags
Which are like million dollars to them
Scrabbling around the floor
Searching for food.

I sit there and think
How their life is different from ours
How they work at the age of 10
And don't get the thrill of a British child's life.

Hayley Dunn (15)
Beauchamps High School, Wickford

Grandma Vera

Sometimes I sit and wonder so
Why my grandma had to go
Every wrinkle every line
Had a story so divine

Her hair was like the morning dew
All grey and frosty and frozen through
She used to laugh she used to sing
I always thought she could do anything

Her eyes were sapphires
Not those of a liar
Her teeth were always shining bright
Clamped together firm and tight

The way she used to shuffle past
Was like a tortoise running fast
She always used to smile and say
'How old are you in the month of May?'

Her house was like a treasure trove
There were ornaments, teddies and lots of old clothes
Puppets, books and photos of old
How many stories her things could have told.

She loved to sit in a chair
And have someone comb her short grey hair
She used to love her nails being done
O how she used to have such fun

Knitting used to be her passion
Sitting in her shop creating her own designer fashions
Once she knitted a scarf and used to say
'The scarf fell off Santa's sleigh.'

How I'll miss my grandma being there
It's left my life so cold and bare
But I'll always love her so
And that memory of her will never go.

Katie Ward (12)
Beauchamps High School, Wickford

Simile Poem

As cold as snow - as soft as goo
As squishy as dough - as hard as a shoe

As round as a ball - as tall as a mountain
As big as a hall - as wet as a fountain

As cute as a dog - as thin as a pen
As ugly as a hog - as fat as a hen

As shiny as gold - as precious as a ring
As disgusting as mould - as royal as a king

As muddy as a mound - as hot as the sun
As crazy as a hound - as tasty as a bun

As black as space - as fast as a rocket
As fine as a lace - as deep as my pocket

As rusty as metal - as refreshing as a pool
As beautiful as a petal - as useful as a tool

As clean as a dish - as playful as a kitten
As slippery as a fish - as warm as a mitten.

Sean McKean (12)
Beauchamps High School, Wickford

Nanny, Nanny

Her eyes like a sparkling diamond
They stand out in a crowd
You can see her a mile away
Her face is like a smiley sun
She smiles like a clown.

Her hair is as spiky as a hedgehog
It makes her look much younger.

She moves across the floor like a snail
Don't touch it because it will hurt
But she still makes a good hot chocolate

Her house has more photos than a photography booth
It looks awful;

She goes up the club
To play darts
Mind out she might be blind
Her chat is so old-fashioned
Her clothes are the same.

Reece Wilson (12)
Beauchamps High School, Wickford

The Heat Of The Sand

The soft wind blows across the sandy earth
Withered branches, black in colour, frame the distance
A screech of birds, the trickle of water
A cry from a child, kneeling beside a stream
Her first sight of the pure cool liquid
A crystal tear of joy, trickles down her dusty face
A clear trail on her cheek is left,
She feels soft hands touch her shoulders,
Her mother's soothing voice is all she hears.

The wind blew her long straggly hair over her eyes,
Her mother knelt beside her, wrapping her shawl tightly,
It was a warm morning, but the wind was sharp,
The sand was blowing in circles around them,
The cool clear water lapping over their hands,
As they collected it in the large clay containers,
The water that they need each day for the necessities in life.

We never had to do this,
It never had occurred,
To me that other people,
Had to do these things in life,
Besides, now I'm in this new world,
I've forgotten all about England.

Kirsty Farrant (15)
Beauchamps High School, Wickford

Culture

Culture is a funny thing
I'm from a colourful, vibrant background
Where nothing is dull
The sun beams down and never lets up

One day something changed, my world fell apart
My being was shattered like shards of glass
From East to West we travelled
Where the sun never shines.

I hadn't even thought about being
Different, not the same, outcast, a freak
From East to West we travelled
Where the sun never shines

My clothes, my religion, my life
Is not accepted. Freedom I crave
From East to West we travelled
Where the sun never shines.

At school we are meant to be the same
However the stares don't stop me for a second
From East to West we travelled
Where the sun never shines.

Charlotte Whiteley (15)
Beauchamps High School, Wickford

New Culture

I walk through the door into the classroom
Beads of sweat rolling down my forehead
Even though I was wearing a uniform,
I felt different.

Everyone in their bright classroom,
Turned their heads to look at me,
I felt like their prey,
And they the predator.

Everyone staring knew I wasn't from England
My hair stuck out a mile
And my skin was a darker shade.

As people asked my name
Different identities ran through my mind
Normal simple names
But I thought I should have no shame

Even though I am different culture
Maybe I can learn about theirs
As they mine.

Zoe Batchelor (15)
Beauchamps High School, Wickford

A Surprise From India

They sent me a wedding dress from India
Unusual coloured silks
Embedded with dazzling jewels
Embossed slippers, silver and red points curling
Like the sidewinder snake
Fashions change in Calcutta
Just like London.

I tried on the beautiful dress
I felt alien glaring in the mirror
As I knew my family had chosen my husband to be.

I longed to be
Just like my English friends
As they got to pick
Unlike me, half Indian
Just like Mum and Dad.

Emma Bailey (15)
Beauchamps High School, Wickford

English Home

From my home
To a place as dry as a bone

A war-torn land
This is nowhere near grand

The smell of death
Takes your breath

I can't understand the ways
Or the days

The dress sense scares
But also has a flair

Strange names
Foreign games

I can't go
But I want to go - home.

Lewis Mansfield (15)
Beauchamps High School, Wickford

The Culture Swap

The move was awful
We were without possessions for weeks
The place was far from joyful
I was sat next to geeks
They were talking all the way
Of megabytes and killer watts
Awake for more than a day
I couldn't give a toss.

Finally we arrived home
Or the house that we lived in now
Mum said it would feel like home
I couldn't think of how
Soon we had unpacked our stuff
And I would go to bed
Quite frankly I had had enough
I needed to rest my head

Two weeks later I felt the same
A few things though which were new
I'd learnt to play a different game
Baseball was a boring thing to do
I couldn't understand some words
Like soccer, trash and mart
The money here is easy though
The dollar or the buck
I start my new high school tomorrow
I can't believe my luck.

My mum says that I'll make new friends
I hope I like it there
I want a nice cruise to the end
I hope that someone cares
One week on and now I'm fine
I understand the terms
I fit in at the school of mine
My new friends help me learn.

Peter Harrison (15)
Beauchamps High School, Wickford

Bombs And Baghdad

They sent a teddy bear
Dusty, faded
And another
Rough and patched as coconut
Mum's knitted socks, black and white,
Fluffy, comfortable
St Christopher gold pendant
Shiny, brand new
Like in England, fashions diminished
Just like school,
The camo leggings were heavy and damp
Smelt stagnant
My brother opted for a sand-beige T-shirt,
Soft linen,
For the sun.

I don't want to stay here
I really don't
The machine guns and bombs
That marauding drone
I want to go home
I want to go home
I can't stand the fighting
The dim battle-plagued lighting.

I'm on a plane, it's not going home
I can still hear that frightful drone
'It's a missile, I really know
The plane's been hit, here I go
The presents they sent, I cherished forever
They won't see me anywhere . . . *never*!'

Max Gammer (15)
Beauchamps High School, Wickford

My Mum

My mum is always there for me
She cooks me tea
And I always have fun
With her mostly when there's a lot of sun
We are a great team together
I'm going to love my mum for ever and ever

She taught me how to walk
And how to talk
My mum has black hair
And is very fair
I think she's the best mum in the world
And she's not very old
And she's never a fool
And is very cool.

She read to me when I was young
And makes sure all my homework's done
These are just a few reasons why
I love my mum!

Shannon Thompson (12)
Bottisham Village College, Cambridge

The Way Of Life

Life is a journey with many passages and tunnels
Hideouts and mazes
Sunlight and Earth
Smooth gentle breezes flowing through the stars
Rushing waves going through the ocean life
Animals and forests growing through the sky
Life as a journey which should never end, tonight.

Stephanie Blanco (13)
Bottisham Village College, Cambridge

Troubled Inside

He needed help . . . his fingerprints over his own gun . . .
The gun prints over his head . . . a gunshot was heard from miles

away . . .

Was he dead?
People say suicide is the way out but was it his?
Maybe . . . maybe not . . .

April Spencer (12)
Bottisham Village College, Cambridge

Football Crazy

Football is really great
I can play with my mates
It really is cool
It really does rule!

I play a match
We score lots of goals
The keeper does a catch
He does lots of rolls!

We might well win
They almost got a goal
The ball hit my chin
Right on the mole

They have lost
Which comes at a cost
We, get medals
And a big cup!

Alex Breeze (12)
Bottisham Village College, Cambridge

Football

Football is a wonderful sport the aim of the game is to score
Pass the ball left to right, play at day and at night
The roar of the crowd, the smell of the dirt
A kick on the shin, ow! That hurt!
Run down the pitch to get the ball
Defender comes in be careful you don't fall
The striker's onside, can he hold his nerve?
Hits the ball with a wonderful curve
Holding our breath, will it go in?
Hits the post, they can always try it again.

Joe Wilson (12)
Bottisham Village College, Cambridge

Unlock

However you wiggle
However you squirm
The magic lock stays firm and firm
However you wiggle however you shake
A magic lock will never break
But only discover the magic key
One click on 'turn' and you'll be free.

Chay Appadoo (12)
Bottisham Village College, Cambridge

Basketball Rhyme

This is my basketball rhyme
Gotta beat the time
Gonna shoot the ball
The crowd think I'm cool

Now my team is all tame
Gotta keep our head in the game
And when we get the rebound
Everyone will hear the sound

Now we have to grab it and go
Put everything in the game that we know
Now we are going to get nothing but net
And after this we will all get wet

Don't do a three in the key
Or else the crowd won't go yippee
If you put it straight in to the hoop
And catch it again you can do the loop

Our stage is known as the court
Too bad some of our players are too short
Too bad they have got good skills
Steroids are the Devil's pills

When the crowd all just shout
Then we know that the time is out
Now we go and get changed
Next time we will get our head in the game.

Addam Morley (12)
Bottisham Village College, Cambridge

The Four Seasons

Spring, summer, autumn, winter
These are the seasons that people sing to
Some are hot and some are cold
And when it's rainy, stories are told

Winter comes and autumn goes
With a runny and cold, wet nose
Making big white snowmen
And snow until half-past ten

Even more strength
The wind blows
Trees have no leaves
And everyone knows

Winter has gone now and spring has come
Animals coming out to have some fun
Blossom growing on the trees
Now everyone can sit on their knees

Playing with the fresh-cut grass
Exams starting and trying to pass
More activities starting at school
And people are even buying a pool

Look out people here comes summer
Summer holidays, kids have done a runner
Nice hot beach, with yellow sand
With little babies just learning to stand.

Here comes autumn,
So find some conkers,
Smashing together,
The children are bonkers.

So there they are,
The seasons flow,
Forever and ever,
The red sun glows.

Hayden Fuller (12)
Bottisham Village College, Cambridge

The Haiku Haiku

Haiku, haiku, yeah!
Haikus are so amazing
Cos they are simple.

Otis Moorman (12)
Bottisham Village College, Cambridge

King Arthur Poem

There once was a king called King Uther
And he had a baby, who was called Arthur
But he wasn't married so he was taken away . . .
But it turned out it was a price to pay . . .

Then a sword stuck in a stone, appeared it read:
'Whoever pulls this out will be King' it said
But then Ken and Sir Ector, they had a thought . . .
And when the other knights came they were totally distraught
Little King Arthur had done it without a thought.

Alex Nicholls (12)
Bottisham Village College, Cambridge

In Your Eyes

As I'm looking in your eyes
All I see is blue
As I stand there staring
I can see that you're all true

As I'm looking in your eyes
All I see is brown
I see you smiling
I know you'll never put me down

As I'm looking in your eyes
All I see is green
And when I lay down at night
You're all that's in my dreams.

Shannon Copare (13)
Bottisham Village College, Cambridge

My First Day At Bottisham Village College

I'm in assembly
Who where all those people?
Will I ever act on the stage?
She has got long brown hair
Where are my friends, Amy, Jenny and Sarah?
Will I remember her name and what she said to us?
I like her earrings, I wonder where she got them
He has got a rip in his jumper, I wonder where he did that
Probably on a bush.
Then Mr Woodman let us go, we all ran out of the double doors
Making a terrible scream.

Amanda Dawson (12)
Bottisham Village College, Cambridge

My First Day At BVC

It's my first day at BVC yay yay yay
Getting up early, getting up early
The sun is out, the sun is out, the sun is out
A bus trip away from home I see one big school
I see big classrooms, strange science labs,
I see one weird plant and a really big strange cafeteria
Must be alien food because there's so much
I see an alien technology calculator
It has so many buttons.
I see a jumble of numbers on a piece of paper
I spot the clock 3:22, ahh that's my home time
Then I remember I was at BVC
Oh the food there when I eat it,
It's better than food from Planet Primary.

Sam Stringer (11)
Bottisham Village College, Cambridge

Secondary School Is Coming!

A billion zillion miles from the bus
Walking slowly towards
It was funny, rectangular and yellow
At school giants loom towards you
Big bags bash your sides
Loads of teachers
Only 6 or 7 back at primary
Silly all the numbers on the doors
Almost terrifying

Classes have started
I'm bunched in the corner
I'm sure the clock has stopped
The speech is droning on and on
But, it's time to move now
Next I'm right up front
The teacher's eyes flick left to right
But soon it'll all be over,
Ahh!

Alice Hubbard (11)
Bottisham Village College, Cambridge

My First Day At Bottisham Village College

A big bus ride from home at to BVC
In assembly listening to Mrs Evans
Her clothes are pretty
I look odd in my uniform
Time for class

Got my organiser
And lunch card
Aaah lunch.

Science is now and I am getting lost,
Oh dear I can't see my buddy!
Good I'm here!
I didn't get too lost . . .
Now a safety video on science

Imagine getting your hair burnt by a Bunsen burner
That wouldn't be funny
Those kids in the video are wearing funny clothes
Yeah! Break time! Whoopee!
Oooh look there's my friend
Wait for me!
Uh-oh where did they go?
Time for tech.

Oh bother I'm lost again
I'm here - textiles time
Mum is doing something now
I wonder what? Sewing perhaps?
Now we dress up stick people
My one looks really funny.
Hee hee!
Yay! Lunch! My favourite class of the day!

Lunch is over. Boo-hoo!
Art and design time
I like drawing it expresses me,
That sounds really cheesy,
A lot of sayings sound cheesy,
I like cheese,
Art over, maths time.

Maths is a bit silly, I reckon
I mean we have calculators, don't we?
Maths over, home time!
Good bye BVC!
See you tomorrow!

Jenny Shelley (11)
Bottisham Village College, Cambridge

First Day At School

Waiting at the bus stop
Waiting for the beast
To pick me up
And drop me off
At the big school
That's like a cathedral
Where big kids rule
And Year 7s look weird
In their new uniforms.

Going into assembly,
Where the head teacher stands,
She looks nice
She talks about discipline
I hope I don't get too much homework
Tomorrow will be harder
The big kids will be there
At the big school
That's like a cathedral.

Sarah Loker (11)
Bottisham Village College, Cambridge

Pearls

The pearls on her neck
Glistening in the sun
Until the clouds come
Along and ruin her fun

The clouds are here
The young girl is in fear
She runs to her pocket
To find her locket

The sun is out
Without a doubt
The girl is outside again

She sits on a wall
But fears she will fall
So she climbs down
And brushes her gown.

Georgia Morris (11)
Bottisham Village College, Cambridge

School

What's going to happen in assembly today?
Is that my friend please say it is
What a lot of information to take in
Phew it's over.

What's going on? Where is my next lesson?
It must be that way.
The next lesson that I've got is English I think
That's my form teacher at the front
Now it's English
(An hour later)
Now it's break time, to meet my friends
Break was fun now it's time for another lesson.

Georgia Hellmers (11)
Bottisham Village College, Cambridge

My First Day At BVC

On my first day at BVC
I got to school
I was scared
I saw new faces
People were looking
Assembly Mrs Evans was talking

What do I do now?
I'm lost, where do I go?
My next lessons started
I think I'm late
Thank goodness I'm not
People started to come out
I'm not late, I'm early
I wonder what my brother's doing now
Is he having fun?
I wonder, I wonder.

Our form did some sums
They were hard
All of the teachers helping me
At the end of the day
What do we have
I couldn't find our car
I wonder if my mum missed me!
I had a great day.

Abi Pain (11)
Bottisham Village College, Cambridge

I'm Dreading The Day

It seems weird getting on the bus
At my primary school I had to walk
It's much more cooler going on the bus
I get to sit next to my friend who's called Connor
Man, you should get on the bus
It's boiling!
At break time everyone crowds to get outside
It's really weird going to different classrooms in lessons.

You should see how many friends I've got now
From different years, I can't believe it
I never knew I would be quite so popular
Everyone walking past in the corridor says,
'Are you a Year 7?
What's your name?' It's really annoying!
I'm getting tired of walking up and down,
But apart from that I love it!

Josh Vowden (11)
Bottisham Village College, Cambridge

My First Day At BVC

At my first day at BVC
I was very nervous
I did not know what to do
Or where to go at all
I thought I'd lost my pencil case
But found it in my bag
I wondered what the teachers would be like
But they all seemed very nice.

Rachel Moore (11)
Bottisham Village College, Cambridge

The Meaning Of Life - Why Are We Here?

Pollution
Terrorists
Weapons of mass destruction
What is the meaning of life?
Fags
Alcohol
Juvenile delinquents
Why are we here?
Drugs
Murders
Kids getting killed
What's it all about?
Robbery
Grand theft auto
Assault
What's the point?
Racism
Armed robbery
Kidnapping
It doesn't have to be this way.

Nathan Wyer (13)
Bramfield House School, Halesworth

The Meaning Of Life

The meaning of life means
To live in the great world which our Lord made
And to find a family to keep your name going
And to find peace in the big wide world
If you don't choose to find peace you will find pain
The world has lots of surprises to find.

And when your life ends you will go to Hell or Heaven.

Jamie Anderson (13)
Bramfield House School, Halesworth

Skinny Or Scary?

Why are all celebs we see
Thin as sticks, it's weird to me
No one's meant to be that way
But no, that's not what the papers say

With bones on show and ribs out wide
It creeps me out, it's wrong inside
We are humans
We're not sticks
Some exposure makes me sick
Young girls who feel they have to be,
Who will be twigs.

Why be that?
Don't you know what the definition of a woman is?

Women are who they want to be,
Not who others choose to see,
Women can look as they like,
Thin's not in,
Girls take a hike!

Antonia Nolan (12)
Breckland Middle School, Brandon

The Wrestler's Ring

The bell sounds *ding ding*
Two wrestlers enter the ring
Everyone looks, a sudden cheer for the almighty
Yet nobody cheers for the small frightened child
Who already has bruises to show for previous fights
Enter the spotlights, focused on the child
Her eyes are glistening and full of tears,
Her face is pale and full of fear,
Looking around for help, nobody goes near
But there is hope as an old lady looks in
She stands at the side thinking, *poor little thing*
She can't help at all
It's far too late
He's started moving towards her
This must be her fate
All she did, was stand up to him for once
Now she wishes she's stayed silent and peaceful,
But then again, as nothing's for sure
If she had nothing, it wouldn't cure
A scream and a bang, she falls to the floor
The crowd stays still and doesn't say a word
They don't tell anyone of the screams they have heard.

It sounds like a wrestling match to you,
But actually it's a father and daughter,
He beats her and hits her,
Who would do that? Who?

Katy Merryweather (13)
Breckland Middle School, Brandon

But Why?

You are the one that made me cry
You are the one that threatened me
But why?

You are the one that punched me
You are the one that called me names
But why?

Now I am the one that made you cry
I am the one that made you run
But why?

Because you bullied me, I made you see
I am just me and that's all I can be,
That's why!

Charlotte Corke (12)
Breckland Middle School, Brandon

The Unspoken

I came in through my door
The shock hit me
As I looked down at the floor
I saw what he was doing
Hitting and kicking
Hurting her bad.

The thing that makes me mad
Is I cannot tell anyone or be a witness,
As I am a cat.
The truth forever will be unspoken!

Francesca Collins (12)
Breckland Middle School, Brandon

Window's Eye

As I stare at the garden all day long
I watch and I wonder what's going on
I have no name for anything
I have no brain or anything

I watch these creatures of all colour
Fly by me and make me shudder
I dream of being one of them
Though I can't I'm just one of life's stems.

Matt Molyneux (12)
Breckland Middle School, Brandon

The Gun

My wings spread in the sky
Although I'm not visible to the naked eye
I swoop down gradually
As silent as the night
My prey is below me
Then with a fright and almighty might
I was hit, down I fall
Lower and lower
I am an eagle, greatest bird of all.

Callum Pritchard (12)
Breckland Middle School, Brandon

The Terrorist

I am the one who made your mum scream
I am the one who ate all your cheese
I am the one who made your cat mad
I am the one who made the birthday boy sad
I went throughout the house chewing and scratching
At brightly coloured paper
But I'm not the one who'll re-wrap them later
I am the one who shredded your best clothes
I am the one who has a sensitive nose
Can you guess, at your very best?
I am a mouse
Give me a rest!

Kirsty Trechsler (13)
Breckland Middle School, Brandon

The Little Child

How old are you?
You look like two
Where is your dad?
Has he been bad?
I've watched you cry
Please do not die
Are you alone?
Here, borrow my phone.

Bethany Pegg (12)
Breckland Middle School, Brandon

Lunar Fantasia

The moon, the moon.
Am I searching for steps not there?
Am I treading on a knife edge
With which I will cut my monthly cheese?
Am I entering untouched lands,
But for the man on the moon I may cease to find?
The moon, the moon.
Am I still dreaming
With pleasure on Earth;
As I stare at it gleaming?

Sam Wood (12)
Comberton Village College, Cambridge

Lottie

Swifter than a thoroughbred
Sleek and shiny, noble head
Biggest, brightest brownest eyes
As if she was always in surprise
With coat of autumn leaves she leaps
Nestled down, nose to tail, as a crescent she sleeps.

Phyllis Armstrong (11)
Comberton Village College, Cambridge

Untitled

Anger. There is no 'saving grace'
Raging, lid-less.
So alarmingly distorted with tears,
I must watch this world through glass bricks
Its light smarting and snagging,
Tearing the corners of eyes.

It has no place in this world
No shape, no form, no 'face value'
    Fie, anger, what would you sell me for?
She will render you powerless;
Watchful, (with torn eyes)
You will feel the scathing of sharp edges
Beneath your skin
    For what price would you set me free?
The scalding of tears.

Emily Conboy (16)
Dr Challoner's High School, Little Chalfont

Elemental

Water:
Waves and currents endlessly there,
Evaporated vapour in the air,
Calm and peaceful the ocean moves,
And all the animals it soothes.

Earth:
Firm and just, yet soft and fine,
Giver of life to trees like pine,
Formation of rock containing prizes,
Through it your spirit rises.

Fire:
Destruction and death follows flame,
To it most point the blame,
It cannot heal only harm,
Burn the skin of any arm.

Air:
Bringer of life and beauty above,
Clouds are ruled by its healing dove,
Allows us to draw breath,
And repels all that is death.

Benjamin Carpenter (12)
East Bergholt High School, Colchester

A Homeless Man

A homeless man sits in a street
With a hungry, old dog sat by his feet
When a little girl comes to greet
A homeless man sat in a street

He pleads, 'Oh young girl can you spare a pound?
I can't stay here lying around.'
'Oh old man I feel your pain
You can't stay here crying in vain.

Here's a coin to find your way
To a warm and comfy place to stay.'

And so he went with joy and laughter
And from then on,
He lived happily ever after.

Samantha Fynes (12)
East Bergholt High School, Colchester

Knife

I despise you
And wish you wouldn't use me as much

Being shoved away
Is my worst nightmare

You use me as your weapon
I wish I could attack you
So you know how it feels

I can't wait until
The day I become blunt

But I'm scared of being thrown away

I feel shut away
I wish I could be displayed.

Kerry Baxter (14)
East Bergholt High School, Colchester

Together Forever

As I look into your eyes
I see stars like diamonds in the sky
As your hand touches mine
I feel your soft silky skin
And it's fine!
As we get a little closer
And our arms bind gently round our bodies . . .
As your lips touch my lips
Our hearts start to skip!

Thinking, dreaming of our lives
Together, forever.

Charlotte Lucas (13)
East Bergholt High School, Colchester

When I'm Not There

When I'm not there you're in trouble
Your dignity depends on me
You use us all
And repay us with nothing
Together me and the others grow smaller day by day
Together we watch each of our own visits
What you consumed the night before
It's us you rely on
But when the time comes
One thoughtless sudden move or sudden rush, panic!
And you will see the sight you hate to see.

Emma Mann (13)
East Bergholt High School, Colchester

I Protect You

I protect you
From things outside
Things you don't want to see
Things you don't need to see

I hope that one day
You will stop pulling so hard at me
The constant back and forwards
No wonder I'm fraying at the edges

I keep you safe at night
So you can dream in secret
You have no worries
While you are in my company.

Ami Baalham (14)
East Bergholt High School, Colchester

A Rolled Up Fag

A rolled up fag sitting in his hand
'Off you go,' he used to say
As I ran through a puff of smoke

Soft. Silky hair ran though his red comb
Hours I sat there brushing his beautiful black hair

You used to come back from the pub
After a pint, go into your room
And have a nap at night,
I sat there waiting for you to awake
And walk through that door.

Needham Market is where you lived,
The only place I remember you.
The last time I saw you,
You lie there in your bed,
With the radio in classic,
'Better get up,' you smiled at me.
Dada finally rose.

Megan Smith (14)
East Bergholt High School, Colchester

Dream

This long extended
Second sings sweetly
For eternity, count
Your thoughts, count
To thirty. Immeasurable
Emotion fills this
Blur of thick
Intensity . . . faces
And gestures cast
Their best into
Pooling integrity
Of my memory . . .
Colours and
Motions
Sweep
My
Eyes
With
Bitter-
Sweet,
Aggressive
Sleep.

Rowan St John (14)
East Bergholt High School, Colchester

My Sis

I remember when you'd collect me from school
Our trips to Maccy Ds were always cool
I remember going swimming with you
Down the green flume but not the blue

I remember the way you'd play fluffy bunnies
So many marshmallows, that was always funny
I remember your laugh and the sparkle in your eyes
I remember at Christmas when we made cakes and mince pies

I remember when you dressed me just like
Scary spice with a hairbrush and mic
I still have the picture of me on that day
With way too much make-up and hair getting in my way

I remember the games we would play
I remember that smile every day
I remember you looking out for me
Your little sis, that will always be

I imagine now that we could chat,
About boys or make-up, stuff like that
I can see us in your creative room
Crying and laughing like sisters do

I miss a lot of things about you
I miss our times together too
I miss having you to hug and kiss
But most of all I miss my sis.

Bethany Welch (15)
East Bergholt High School, Colchester

The Cat

As the morning sun breaks
He appears out of the mist
His black fur moist with dew
His pink shining nose
He prowls like a lion
Down the path
Breaking into a run
As he hears 'food'
With the speed of a cheetah
He races down the path
Into the kitchen and within
A blink of an eye
The food has gone.

Josh Harrison (13)
East Bergholt High School, Colchester

Personification

I wake up in the morning
I see you for hours
Getting ready to go out
I brush my hair, you brush yours
You do exactly the same
Then you go, I go
It's quiet.

I am just the background,
The walls, the part of your bed
I always wondered how the other half looked
But I can't see round that far

I see you again, you walk past together
It's like we're twins. Identical
I don't know what I'd do without you.

Abi Southworth
East Bergholt High School, Colchester

Imprisoned In A Sphere

A band reminiscing with the lyrics of the past
A blue morning's sky holding the door open for planes to pass through
An empty beer can containing chaos of last night's celebrations
And the little light bulb with the capacity to light a room.

A zealous ring placed on a pale finger holding a couple together
A mouth unlocking words, word by word, that could change the face of history,
A sparkling sun-shone ocean, holding a planet underneath and balancing one above,
And the little purse holding coins that could change someone's smile.

A microphone containing a library of voices
A camera storing time
The big brown envelope holding fradious life-changing information
And the little packet of Maltesers containing a social celebration.

The band, the blue morning's sky, the empty beer can,
The little light bulb, the zealous ring, the mouth, the sparkling sun-shone ocean, the little purse, the microphone, the camera, the big brown envelope and the little packet of Maltesers locked in a big prison named the *Earth*!

Sophie Smith (14)
East Bergholt High School, Colchester

Shrubland Hall

It was gigantic, bold and glamorous
Sheep scattered everywhere
It was saturated with everything a rich man could have craved
Inside gardens, tennis courts, swimming pools

It was the 1500-acre estate
The huge lake sat beside the forest
To stay the night
The famous paintings hung up like nobody realises that
It's actually there.

It was the opening
Hiding the pathway to freedom
Leading to the castle like mansion
It was the massive stairs followed by a gigantic fountain.

It was the well kept stone bricked wall
Blocking off fascination
The generations that a family have lived there
Now they're gone!

Joseph Stevens (14)
East Bergholt High School, Colchester

Dance

As the spotlight brightens
And the music begins
I'm up on my toes
And I'm ready to spin

I jump and I leap
From one side to another
Feeling the rhythm
Like no other.

To dance is my dream,
I can't let it die,
For when I do dance,
I feel I can fly.

The world can disappear,
Dancing is my release,
For just that moment,
I'm truly at peace.

Natalia Vidal (13)
East Bergholt High School, Colchester

Nellie

Nellie you were so kind
Every penny you owned you gave away
I wish I could have visited you much more
In your humble abode you welcomed every type of folk
Your happy laugh would light up the neighbourhood

A church goer you were
A social lady, the wise owl of the village
You never once forgot my birthday
Only now, being older, do I really appreciate that
I hear your laugh, echoing, singing with the birds.

The sound of your sticks outside told us you were fine
As you slowly made your way to the outside bathroom
Your house, plain and simple but always full of love
Kindness radiated like the warm flames of your coal fire
That's you laughing underneath the silver birch?

Nobody else I know loved children more
Always ready to listen to my tales with a kindly word
And offering me juicy blackberries you picked with care
How I wish you had reached the age of 93
That chuckle is still around, I'm sure.

Something else died that night you fell asleep for good
The very essence of the village, you were Weeley
My first time at a funeral, wow the church was packed!
Now I often cycle up to see you in your perfect resting place
Your laugh I heard so often will never be forgotten.

James Olley (15)
East Bergholt High School, Colchester

The Good Life

Do you remember us stroking your nose?
You used to love it but never anywhere else

You always slept in the same spot
Half in the sun, half in the shade
Not stirring until dinner time!

And even then you still had your preferences
Tinned food without any of the dry stuff
I will always remember you as my first pet, small and fluffy
I recall Mum and Dad telling me how you came home,
Covered in fleas, sitting snugly in Dad's palm

The last time I saw you, you were ready to die
Perched on your chair as sad as can be,
But still with a glint in your eye.

Matthew Springett (15)
East Bergholt High School, Colchester

A Place I Remember Well

It was massive, dominant, grand
It was made of solid brick stone
It was the statues which surrounded the front façade
Making everyone see how grand it was.

It was the marble staircases, the crystal chandeliers
And the long narrow hallways.
It was the lobby, the jewels, and the gold
Making the room shimmer with light
It was the royal chapel, keeping watch of the city, and protecting it
It was the statues clinging to the ceiling, threatening anyone who enters

It was defined by the water, which has surrounded it
It leads me to the key of the country
It has a massive obelisk
A courtyard with threatening guards ready to kill

It was the most dominating building in the city,
Sprawling far and wide
It was the most powerful building there, both historically and
economically
It was the most well protected, with guards
Surrounding every entrance, armed and ready.

Mark Brands (14)
East Bergholt High School, Colchester

A Different Picture

A pen not very exciting, but it might make a difference
A galaxy where the stars live their life
A whole world that keeps us happy
A pond full of little fish swimming about

A garden full of flowers that make you happy
A flower full of colours that make your day
A house full of people that you all love

A pan full of food that will feed the starving
A theme park that gets your heart racing
A universe full of planets and other life
A computer full of software, what a help.

Katie Nunn (13)
East Bergholt High School, Colchester

My Eyes

To wake up one morning
To the sound of the
End of a life
Is the worst thing
In the world

You walk down to find
The most significant
Man in your life gone

Suddenly,
The birds stop singing
The wind stops blowing
The taste of warm
Toast in the morning may
As well be wood

My eyes stare into the distance
Trying to believe the tragedy
My eyes blank
My eyes vacant
My eyes gone
No point in living
No point in dying
I am still here, but he is not.

Della Massey (14)
East Bergholt High School, Colchester

Addiction

First fame in nineties
And people partied
And they danced
And they chatted, and they can't stop

I swallowed and I coughed
But then I could dance, I could dance all night
Colours intensified, people blurred
I felt at home, I felt at home
But I couldn't stop

Then I felt dizzy
Dizzy
Jaw tight, pain
Pain rushing down me
Inside me
Taking me
Killing me
But I couldn't stop

So I swallowed and coughed
Then I felt happy, warm, emotional
With energy, buzz, buzz!
And I couldn't stop.

Then I felt angry sad alone
Heart problems
Liver problems

Class A, illegal item
But no one cares
No one cares for me

I am alone

And I can't stop.

Jessica Portway (14)
East Bergholt High School, Colchester

Rodents Of The Night

Small feet lay hiding in a chamber
A rotting smell filling their noses
As the fragile grim reapers scuttled about
A heavy breathing started
Deserted in the space
Then the darkness fell
Death had been successful
Killing once more

A letter from the alphabet address across the door
This warned the living
That this person was no more
'Bring out your dead'
Rattled through the streets
Echoes of death
From those tiny feet.

Shannan Wright (14)
East Bergholt High School, Colchester

My Car

My dad has a car
A very nice car
With big wide wheels
They shine like the sun

It is a hatchback
And the colour is black
As dark as the night sky

The roar from the engine
Makes a sound like a lion
You can hear it from far away

One day I will have a car like that
And I will roar through town.

James Hobson (13)
East Bergholt High School, Colchester

Uluru

It was huge!
Massive, red and
In the centre of nowhere
It seems more than a rock, more sacred.

It was surrounded by a vast
Blood-red desert plains
Sitting there
Like a god's throne, or tomb

It was riddled with
Many caves
Where the wonderful pictures of the Dreamtime reside,
Ancient home of the Aborigines.

It was the sacred icon of the Anangu tribe.
Not only does it sum up itself,
It sums up Australia,
A magnificent, sacred, holy place.

It was Uluru.

Josh Osborne (13)
East Bergholt High School, Colchester

Old Trafford

It was Old Trafford
Not old not grey
No old bricks or nothing
Just hard, strong steel

It was a place of luxury
A place where stars lived
A place where people get paid
Ridiculous amounts of money

It was a huge place in fact
Lots of seats, white and red

It was great to be skulking there
Where great footballers once walked
Where people have come through the
Hallway where people have shed blood
And where a man of great power
And legend football skills once walked
George Best! Who ruined his life
Through alcohol.

Stewart Ashfield (13)
East Bergholt High School, Colchester

It Was

It was green very green
Grass as high as I could see
The trees towered over my three-year-old self

It was a winding path
Full of gravel, of stone
Grass to either side went on and on

It was defined by simplicity
How beautiful it was
Nothing man-made to spoil it

Too good for me
It was a long time ago
And I have already forgotten.

Josh Overton (13)
East Bergholt High School, Colchester

What Am I?

I'm alone at the crack of dawn
The peace is fractured at your wake
You leave
I'm left alone

I sit alone and still
Just waiting for you
You're like a hot water bottle
So warm and huggable

But now the sun is gone
You're back
I'm happy to hold you
And rock you soothingly to sleep.

Steph Mayhew (13)
East Bergholt High School, Colchester

The Riddle Poem

Half a year I sleep unnoticed
Yet when there's need you feed me
The decapitated remains of the sprout of the earth
I can always see thee

As my reign begins with heat
So it shall continue
After you left me last year
I have wanted you

How I mesmerise and hypnotise
Has never been a secret
I need food, you need heat
We can never leave it

I am forever hungry
For the sorrow shoots that kindle
I am death, I am murder
For the green armies that dwindle

But as my time again draws to a close
I thinking, feeling
That one day we will be together
To me you will be kneeling.

Piers Harrison-Reid (13)
East Bergholt High School, Colchester

Grandad

You could see your curly hair from a mile off
It was the only thing Lucy was gentle with
Remember the time when you wore a doll's jumper on your head?
We laughed our heads off our hours afterwards.

The last time I saw you, you'd had a haircut
Although you said, 'I went to the barbers,' which I didn't understand.
You had a bald spot on the back of your head
I remember that Lucy and me laughed
When she said that one day Dad would get one too.

And you came to Lucy's birthday party,
She must've been quite young,
But I remember taking a photo: 'Say cheese, Grandad!'

Oh yeah, and we had the same glasses, Grandad,
D'you remember that?
I liked being the same as you.

Laura Lovelock (13)
East Bergholt High School, Colchester

Loneliness

I just lie there in a dark cupboard
Waiting for you to suffocate me
Then drown me in water and liquid
The only time I see you is when you open the door
And how I love that moment I get to breath,
But then 'splat' it's all over
I'm suffocating under your food
'Scrape', your knife digs into me
Hot food burns me and you don't help me
Finally I can breath again
All the food is cleared off my face
But I know what's going to happen next
Dunk in the water
Wiping across my face
I can't breath I'm drowning
At least I'm out
But not for long
Back in the dark cupboard
Soul-destroying loneliness.

Georgina Gray (13)
East Bergholt High School, Colchester

He's In Control

I see you every day
Staring at my face
And I stare back at yours

I show you everything you want to see
I bring you love, excitement and joy
All at the same time

But every night you leave me
You lock me away in a dark, deserted cave
Where I rust and dream of you

It's the same routine every single day!
But one day I will have you
One day we will be together

I will lock you up with me
You will no longer be in control of me
I will be in control of you.

Thomas Maddams (13)
East Bergholt High School, Colchester

Crantock

It was magical, my view
Soft white sand, for miles and miles
The fresh green reeds, the backbone of the beach
The salty gannel speeding towards the sea

The house was quite modern but with that relaxed edge
A solid wooden table
And the huge comfy sofa

It was defined by a small crumbly wall
And a cliff
With the sea sweeping on and on

It was so special that place
The flower on the rose
A one in a million.

Grace Hudson (13)
East Bergholt High School, Colchester

I Remember

I remember visiting you on top of the hill overlooking the bay. I remember listening to your old gramophone, to your best tunes time and time again.

Going down to the sea front was good fun, up and down the beach and then on the pier.

'The dog must learn,' you would say as well as 'thank you love', was often heard.

'She did like her cards,' Grandma still says.

The last time I saw you, you were in hospital, we took you into the garden and we all had your birthday cake, you were truly happy.

We love your house.

It was solid, hard as stone, never changing. Holding up two flags, waving in the air, the big grey roads, the flower-covered house, waving in the wind.

Cold inside, hot out.

Formal, yet comforting.

Always happy.

Large wooden shutters.

Peeking out into the town.

The cup that cannot ever be emptied,
The muddle of a small cosy cottage,
The shine of the crown, always grand
The soldiers of the castle, never defeated
The juggler in his grave,
The repetiveness of the can, always used.
The rust of the kettle in the corner.

Jack Tooze (13)
East Bergholt High School, Colchester

Grace!

I remember you Grace
When we were best friends
From those first scary days at school
When we took along our familiar toys
My rabbit, your bear - for comfort
Sitting side by side
We soon became very close.

I remember when after school
We used to share our homes
Taking it in turns to provide fun and games
And also the times, we spent in your mum's florists
Amongst the colours so pretty and bright
Remind me now of the times that I miss

I remember the times that we raced and had fun
We used to laugh, and we used to joke
In the clover-filled playground
Not wanting ever for the bell to ring
We used to tell each other
That we should never part
That we would be friends forever

I remember one day you said you were moving
And the time that we parted on the last day of term
Your sad face, in the window of the departing car,
We said we would meet again
And stay in touch,
But we both made new friends,
I remember you often,
You and your bear!

Sarah Frost (13)
East Bergholt High School, Colchester

I Long For

I long for the winters
You're near all the time
I want you close to me
But you can't come near
I flicker away inside
As my friends slowly die down

I'm no use in summer
You reject me
I'm alone left cold and still
You'll want me back again
You will I know
My fiery impressive dance
Will draw you back
I'm lifeless without you
My dust will draw me to leave with the wind
I'm stronger than you think.

Siân Llewelyn (13)
East Bergholt High School, Colchester

What Am I?

I used to get excited when you approached me
You sent a shiver down my spine as you reached to pick me up
I used to bubble up inside as you touched me
You made me feel hot all over
But now I feel old and used
I cringe when you come near
You still make me feel hot all over when you touch me
But not in a good way
I'm exhausted from when you use me all the time
And I'm sad knowing that you use me until I die!

Stephanie Goodwin (13)
East Bergholt High School, Colchester

Autumn

A corns close up and drop off all the trees
U p above the trees birds fly high
T rees blow sweetly in the wind
U nder the leaves lies a fluffy white bunny
M uddy paths all over the place
N othing better than autumn.

Paige Simpson (11)
Ferrers Specialist Arts College, Higham Ferrers

Autumn

Autumn when the fire is roaring
Days are darker
Leaves are falling

Dewy grass
Webs hung like lace
Woolly mittens
Rosy face

Leaves turn gold
Red then brown
Tumbling, falling
Smoother the ground

In the middle of the forest
Stands the tall proud pine
His coat of fragrant fingers
How he looks so fine.

Lucy Groom (11)
Ferrers Specialist Arts College, Higham Ferrers

Jessica

Whenever I need her
She is always there
We are stuck like glue
I know I will always need her
She is that special person in my heart

When I am alone
And no one was there
She was always there
When I needed her
When I cry she will
Always cuddle me until I stop crying
She will always know
That I will always be here for her
Even when I'm gone.

Louisa Allen (12)
Ferrers Specialist Arts College, Higham Ferrers

Lampard

He likes to win all the games
He looks so fit and looks great in his kit
He makes England shine every time when he gets a goal
I think he is the greatest of them all
You can always rely all the time on him to take the shot
He is football crazy.

Emily Underwood (12)
Ferrers Specialist Arts College, Higham Ferrers

Football

Football
Peter Crouch is tall
But he's not very cool
When he's playing pool
Turn off your TV
Get up from the couch
Everybody
Let's do the Crouch!

McClaren is ready for his first game
Win at all costs is his aim
Or he'll get the cane
And he will be in a lot of pain!

Ronaldinho is on the ball
He is the coolest of them all
He took a shot
And it was very hot
And the baby went in the cot.

Kieren Taylor (12)
Ferrers Specialist Arts College, Higham Ferrers

Battlefield

B odies thrown into pits of mud
A ngry men grieving over lost soldiers
T he smells of dead bodies rotting on the floor
T he sounds of the battlefield filling everybody with fear
L osing family and friends never seeing them again
E xplosions in the background lighting the land like a light bulb
F ear of screaming people in terror
I llness infecting the healthy and killing the sick
E nthusiastic men heading off to fight
L ying dead on the cold, rocky ground
D ay after day fighting for their proud countries.

Edward Munt (14)
Ferrers Specialist Arts College, Higham Ferrers

Battlefield

B ombs falling as hailstones would on a winter's day
A ll the wide open field ruined by footprints stomped into
T anks and trenches are the only surroundings
T ime is of the essence when you're fighting for your country,
don't disappoint her
L and mines exploding like popcorn in a microwave
E verybody losing their lives around me
F ighting for your lives and your friends
I njuries and illness as far as the eye can see
E nough soldiers to fill a football pitch
L oved ones wait for news
D eath comes to everyone.

Sam Macavoy (13)
Ferrers Specialist Arts College, Higham Ferrers

Battlefield

My first feeling was fear
I would rather sit with a beer
I was due to go home on the ninth
But no one gets what they want in life
Bombs going off everywhere
On the battlefield it's just one big dare
Life is disappearing before my eyes
Before you know it soldiers die
I wish in my arms was my son
But instead I carry a gun
All I see in the air is smoke
Poor boy's gas mask is broke
People hiding under sand bags
All over the floor people's dog tags
In this people's war so many killed
Soldiers get home parents' dream fulfilled.

Rikki Treadwell (13)
Ferrers Specialist Arts College, Higham Ferrers

Forgotten

The tears in my eyes don't always glisten
And the pain wasn't always there
But that doesn't mean I've forgotten
Or I haven't remembered to care

The sorrow in my face doesn't always show
Or the hurt that lies in my heart
But that doesn't mean that I've forgotten
That we're so far apart

The memories don't always come
Sometimes I can't stop fretting
But that doesn't mean that I've forgotten
Only that I'm forgetting.

Elizabeth Elliott
Ferrers Specialist Arts College, Higham Ferrers

Soldier

My gun is aimed, ready, I am just fifteen
Yet here I am on the battlefield
Was it my destiny to kill?
Where is peace, my life is blood spill
Can I do it? Be strong. Pull the trigger hard
The bullet has gone, soaring like an eagle, in the air, into his heart
I have done it, I have murdered
God forgive me, curse the battlefield
And then, behind me a lunge from a sword
Straight through my back - hot blood -
This is the end of my world
My mother will be waiting for me to come home
I never will now, I cannot, she is alone.
Under the pain I am forced to kneel
My hand clenches around my gun
Cold metal, the last thing I will ever feel.

Victoria Williams (11)
Ferrers Specialist Arts College, Higham Ferrers

Bees Buzzing

B eautiful bees buzzing by
E ating nectar as they fly by
E very little buzzing bee
S leep in their hive so peacefully

B ut when they wake again next day
U pon the sky so far away
Z ipping
Z ooming
I n your flowers
N ow they will collect the pollen
G oing to their hives until spring does finally arrive!

Amy Kempster (11)
Ferrers Specialist Arts College, Higham Ferrers

Macey

Macey is my little dog
She's black and white and very sweet
When I'm at school she sleeps like a log
And when I get home she nibbles my feet

She has lots of toys
Her favourite is a rubber duck
She likes the girls but not the boys
She likes to eat but cannot cook

Walkies is her favourite time
She loves to run in the park
She runs off her lead just fine
Finding hedgehogs in the dark.

Amy Kelly (11)
Ferrers Specialist Arts College, Higham Ferrers

The Story

He's fun
Although
He cannot
Run, he is a
Free spirit
Who cannot
See he is my
Brother.
A world of imagination
With dragons, knights
Castles and kings these
Are a few of his favourite
Things.
I push him in his wheelchair
He laughs and enjoys his ride
I am his eyes, I read to him
He is content, he is my brother
That's my brother
Daniel.

Naomi Boxall (11)
Ferrers Specialist Arts College, Higham Ferrers

Winter

The snow glistens
Like stars in a night sky
People sitting in their homes
Eating warm mince pies
As winter only comes once a year
It fills people's hearts, full of cheer.

Robbie Wilkins (12)
Ferrers Specialist Arts College, Higham Ferrers

The Crocodile And The Frog

No animals are half as vile
As the croaky frog and crocodile
Both as big as Big Ben
As they love to crunch
Ten kids and juicy flies for lunch
Both as round as footballs
They love to eat lots and lots
Especially mums and kids and even tots
But one day they ate too much
And couldn't fit into the giant hutch
And that was the end of their eating lives
No animals are half as vile
As the croaky frog and the crocodile!

Jade Lain (11)
Ferrers Specialist Arts College, Higham Ferrers

Autumn

A corns fall from the trees
U ndercoats worn by the cold people
T rees blowing in the cold wind
U nderneath the fallen leaves lays the ground
M uddy grounds please young children
N othing beats autumn!

Molly O'Dell (11)
Ferrers Specialist Arts College, Higham Ferrers

The Scars Under The Lies

My life is crashing before my eyes
Can't take fate
Can't take your lies
Want to break free from this dark, gloomy lair
Fly out on the black wings of my future
The stars sparkled in the midnight sky
Like your eyes
Bright and beautiful
Your soul is a magical place
But killed me unexpectedly
Life took its unexpected turn
You engulfed my soul
And watched it burn
Such pain from such an innocent creature
Took me into the depths of Hell
Burnt my soul
Took all life I ever owned
From all this pain and suffering
A spark still remains
Not understanding why my heart was still calling your name
But I realised it was telling me I still love you
More than words can say
A feeling so powerful
I cry at the thought of life without you
Because I love you
And I shall never stop
You're all I want in life
My past, present and the only future I can see.

Siân Hammond (13)
Hadleigh High School, Ipswich

No Trace

The only fond memory in my head
Is that of a single snowstorm
The snow started to fall
Twirling and dancing like a great ballet

I walked across the great black surface
And looked up towards the sky
I wished I was up there
I wished I might die

A single snowflake landed on my cheek
Burning on my face
It ignited my soul
However I have no soul no trace

I looked out across a great distance
I lived here this place
I turned and looked at the snowflakes
They twisted and turned with such grace

And there it stood so cold and dead
The orphanage
My home

The ballet ended
I was now alone
I had made my decision

I was going to leave this place
There would be no sign of me, no trace.

Lucy Mackie (13)
Hadleigh High School, Ipswich

Fatal Fatness

I'm just a bit corpulent
Elephant-like
They call me podgy
They call me plump
Just because I have an extra thick layer of blubber
But they don't see it like that
They call me 'Flubber'
It's just a little problem
But really it's big just like me
I love my McDonald's
My Burger King
But on Sunday it's KFC
I hate them all
I blame them all
They make me fat
But how can I resist
Great taste and great advertising
But then at school my life is still hell
The names come out and they call me 'beefy'
But sometimes 'chicken'
I hate my life I just want to die
But if I was to die there would be no pie
So I carry on just for them
I want to marry a Big Mac!

Matt Grimwade (13)
Hadleigh High School, Ipswich

Untitled

'What a goal!'
Screams the crowd
Hoping one day that will be me
But instead I sit on the bench
Waiting to be brought on

My birthday comes
I get a new football
Hoping, hoping
One day I can play
Wishing, wishing
To play on the TV
Dreaming, dreaming
I will be great.

Ross Bray (13)
Hadleigh High School, Ipswich

My Dream

When I was young
I had a dream
Playing for Ipswich
At Portman Road
I ran after the ball
Round the keeper
And scored a goal
There I was standing there
With the north stand going mad
There I was at half-time
Drinking a cup of tea
Making myself look sad
Went to the pitch and scored again
Making the other team look bad
There I was scoring yet again
Putting myself in history
As a 13-year-old scoring 3 goals
Against Norwich
That was my dream

I hope you enjoyed it.

Ryan Wood (13)
Hadleigh High School, Ipswich

Who Am I?

Who am I? Who am I? Who am I?
Once I was full of warmth and laughter
But now I'm cold and surrounded by disaster
I was given a chance but now it's gone
I'm lonely, I'm cold, and I'm scared

Once I was given bones to chew
But now I'm left with scraps that of few
My fur is wet and I miss my bed
What did I do to deserve this?

I see figures in front of me not knowing I am there
I wish I had an owner that would care
I saw my face full of fleas
What would be my fate?

I slowly walked down the crooked path
Like I was the king of animals
I saw the light from the homes ahead
But still I wish that I was dead

Who am I? Who am I? Who am I?

Ryan Clemson (13)
Hadleigh High School, Ipswich

In The Autumn

In the autumn the sky is not quite blue
And the grass is not quite green
But in-between the grass and sky
Is the golden glow where summer has been
The golden glow fades to brown
While trees wave in the whistling wind
And then the leaves come falling down
Birds fly off somewhere warm
Brown leaves flutter to the ground
Like butterflies at the end of spring
Then with a quiet crackling sound
Squirrels pounce across the autumn leaves.

Zoe Alleyne (13)
Hadleigh High School, Ipswich

Hags Vs Fawns

The dark ones are always hunting
They are always killing
They are the hags
They come with fire
They come with axes
Biting
Hacking
Chopping
Burning

But then the fawns come
They are the wise ones
They are helpful
They drink and laugh and have parties
They are kind
And they are growing their trees and plants
They are bright.

Adam Higgins (12)
Hadleigh High School, Ipswich

Autumn

The forest was golden
On that wonderful day
The smell was like oak trees
And the sky was blue grey

The leaves were crisp
Above and below
The babbling stream
Clear like a window

The soft crunch of leaves
Was the only sound
And when I stopped walking
A silence was found

And then from the treetops
A birdsong burst free
Brightening the day
And sending hope to me.

Ashley De Banks (13)
Hadleigh High School, Ipswich

The Fall

I'm lying here on the floor
Oh why did I climb
But now no more

Blood is layered on my face
It trickles down my throat
But I only see dark space

I now look back to the previous day
I did not know
The price I now pay

Oh how I hope I'm not ruined forever
But now I think
My whole life will differ

The summer days I spent up there
So warm and crisp
So very aware

Oh how I wish
I could go back in time
And never do this stupid climb

The crack of a branch
Is all it took?
To make this how I'll always look

A dare I say
Or maybe a game
This is what I'll always blame

A blue flash of light and sirens hum
All haunting my senses
And rumbling the ground like a drum

I'm lying here in the ground
Oh why did I climb?
But now not a sound.

Yolanda Rankin (13)
Hadleigh High School, Ipswich

In Hiding

I lurk in the hedges
I run in the moonlight
And I rest in the day
'Pest' they call me
And traps they set after
The mere sight of me
I run and run
From a fate worse
Than death and
If I were to be
Caught I would soar up
Higher than the sky
And squeak in an unheard
Voice, 'goodbye'.

Michael Rose (13)
Hadleigh High School, Ipswich

Spot

The lady who lives down the road
Has a cat that is shaped like a toad
The cat's name is Spot
The lady's called Dot
And their love for each other, it showed.

They went to the park one day,
And there were games Spot wanted to play,
The lady said, 'No!'
Spot threatened to go
And with that he ran far away.

It started to get rather dark
Spot decided this wasn't a lark
A car whizzed by
Like an enraged fly
Startled, Spot returned to the park.

He passed a pond on the way
A frog that jumped out said, 'Good day.
You look just us
So don't get on that bus
Just come swim the whole night away.'

Soaked wet poor Spot was very sad,
He knew he should not be so bad,
When a voice yelled out, 'Kitty!'
His plan had been witty
And Dot hobbled over most glad.

Rebecca Le Grice (13)
Hadleigh High School, Ipswich

Unhappy Child

Walking into a world of rough
Wilderness, I notice things around
Me changing, from being one
Person to another, but why?
I have no answer. Questions I
Am asked, but can't speak their
Meanings are being pumped into my head,
Repeating themselves into my dreams.

Writing . . . but for no reason, just a past time of my thoughts
They all merge together and needing to break out,
They might not mean anything but they reveal
Me from the clutters they have made.
From my words I could write a book,
Not of fiction and also not of facts,
But of mind.
Not of anybody else's mind
But my mind!

Vicky White (13)
Hadleigh High School, Ipswich

Graffiti Artist

Click, clack, spray
Inspiration and colours fill my head
Flowing down my arm into the can
Then out onto the wall
For the world to see
Colour after colour jumping to the wall
Its beginnings are starting to show
All of the colours you can think of
And so much more
The intricate lettering
Like a spider's webbing
The can's hissing like a snake
Shadows swirl around
But I don't notice
I'm at one with the art
So close to being finished
Empty cans fall as fresh are picked up
My wrists are aching
I stand back to admire
To some I'm a vandal
To others I'm an artist
My greatest piece yet
Just wait till tomorrow
I walked off disappearing
Into the flickering street lights
Click, clack, spray.

Ben Hart (14)
Hadleigh High School, Ipswich

Secrets

I have a secret deep inside
A secret that I have to hide
I lie to people who should care
My deepest secret I will not share
The signs are there for all to see
Of what I have become to be
Upon my wrist are scarlet lines
But no one has read my hidden signs

People ask why I'm so shy
But no one knows the reason why
No one knows why I'm so scared
But it's because nobody cares,
As blood trickles down my swollen arm,
I ask myself why cause this harm,
I have a secret deep inside,
A secret that's not so long to hide.

Melissa Parker (13)
Hadleigh High School, Ipswich

Here Is The Sun Of My Life

Gloomy and dull
But there's still lots of life around
Thousands and millions of creatures swarming the ground
Little oasis and hallucinations

I can see a T-rex
But when I close my eyes and open them the T-rex is gone
When I am here I feel as if I am in a swimming pool
All warm and the slightest bit of sound

Here is the sun of my life!
Rrrr rrrr went the engine of the start of the racing season
Unfortunately there came the noise again!

Kate Loder (12)
Hadleigh High School, Ipswich

The Dolphin

The dolphin voice is squeaky like a mouse
But as soft as a pillow
Its slippery snail skin trickles off water
Back into the dark, deep ocean

It's beautiful as a grey dark elephant
But as wild as a cheetah
She loves the sea her big pool, her village,
Her home!

Jodie Smart (12)
Hadleigh High School, Ipswich

Flesh And Bone

Eyes poised still
Teeth ready to eliminate me
Its dark, gloomy shadow gaining on me
Teeth as sharp as iron

Jaw gasping for action
Eyes glaring rapidly
Teeth blasting through bone
Bone smashing up

Eyes bloodstained red
Arms clawing through trees
Legs running like a rocket
Teeth as dirty as a volcano

Teeth grinding together
Claws snapping trees
Teeth as pointed as knives.

Ayrton Artiss (11)
Hadleigh High School, Ipswich

Fish

Swimming, swirling, like rays of light
Flashing in the star of daytime
Floating above in the shining porthole
Connecting you to the world
The ocean of deep, dark emptiness sucking you in
Life or death.

As the killer sways along the bottom
They stop, they die
They don't stop, they die

A fish is a journey,
From life to death,
Swimming in the hell-hole of the ocean,
Is it real or just a hallucination?

As the great predator swims closer;
Each second you worry,
Then as you become a group,
It goes,
Never coming back.

Abigail Slade (12)
Hadleigh High School, Ipswich

Eruption

It is a delicate disaster
It is a colourful blow
The anger of God let loose
Straight from the hell below

The lava is a spill of red paint on a grey background
The white and green lights of the highway
Can't compare to the inferno flames of the devastating mountain

Etna may mean burning
And the mountain once more shows why.

Frazer Last (11)
Hadleigh High School, Ipswich

The Rocky

Miniature mountains in the distance, mask the hostile skies
I cannot see the sapphire heavens which comes as no surprise
With the dense, dusty clouds, covering the roaring sun
But the sun is still trying to tear out like teeth through a bun

The ragged rocks in the floor are really hard to miss
But underneath there might be something that always says 'hiss'
I can only make out rocks as far as I can see
But there is something in the distance which looks like a tree
But I don't think it is, it must be a mystery.

Harrison Boote (12)
Hadleigh High School, Ipswich

The Black Hunter

Piercing red eyes appear from the water
Fishes flee in fear
The animal leaps and
Snap!

Blood trickles through the water
Bones crack as the sun falls
Did you hear that?
Someone's in the forest
And their nature is to kill

Hairs prick up
Noses begin to wobble
Man is in the forest
Run! Run!
The animal is gone . . .

Billie Tearney (11)
Hadleigh High School, Ipswich

Auroras

A magical variety
Of shapes and colours dance
In the sky
As the solar wind buffets Earth's magnetic field
A green ribbon waves
In the icy winter air
The whole dome of the night sky is awash with colours
Sheltered by a rosy curtain of inspiration
It's the heart of a flower
Glorious light whose petals ripple in the breeze
It's the centre of the world
It's the Earth's grand show.

Hannah Maxwell (12)
Hadleigh High School, Ipswich

Winter

The harsh cold holds its ground
As the sun tries to break the thick frost
But when the sun is gone
He digs his pearl-white teeth in further
His hands clasp the throat of life and strangles it
To its death
The winter's here and the sun is gone.

Emma Jackson (12)
Hadleigh High School, Ipswich

My Cliff Side Poem

Baby-blue waves erode clay
Enriched cliffs
White foam dances on the surface

Tide in tide out
Watch the waves roll in

Steep crisp rocks drowning in the
Deep, dark sea tipped back and
Forth and gradually drops and
Sits and rots

Tide in tide out
Don't let it draw you in.

Gemma Bloomfield (12)
Hadleigh High School, Ipswich

The North American Woodpecker

Bird building in rotting trees
Carving out their niche
Making a hollow in which to live

Wings snap open like a bamboo fan
A flicker
A flash of gold

Like a sentry on lookout
Monitoring the sky for predators,
And around the trees as well,
Checking for squirrels just to make sure.

A cold but gentle Alaskan breeze,
Whistling through the groaning trees.

Sam Taylor (12)
Hadleigh High School, Ipswich

Alligator

Long, green and scaly
Their belly is bleached
Their tail is like a thrashing whip
Their body armour hard as rock
Sturdy as a titanium tank
On land they are a rocket on wheels
In water they are a speeding blur
They dive in with a splash
Something caught its deadly sharp eyes
Something's going to painfully die
Clamped in those jaws of steel
They come alive with a fiendish grin
Snap!

Jacob Ebbs (12)
Hadleigh High School, Ipswich

The Graveyard

Forbidden to any life
Derelict
Grey and depressing
Sad and neglected like a graveyard
Broken pointed swords still and lifeless
Once a leafy grove
But now
Dead branches like skeletons, reaching up into the motionless mist
No sound
Plop, the first raindrop of the season
Deep murky waters, holding untold secrets
Stark images reflecting on the rippled water
Deadly sky
Forbidden to any life.

Emily Lewis (12)
Hadleigh High School, Ipswich

War And Peace

War has started, destruction has happened quickly as lightning
Death has started growing by the seconds
Death happens as fast as a baby being born

Bombs fly over the trenches
It's a fast Formula 1 car
Killing is a storm coming every second
Invading countries to own land
What rightfully isn't theirs.

Darkness is very scary it's dark as someone
Closing their eyes about to go to sleep
Misery happens most of the time in wars
Because someone has lost a very important person in their lives.

Peace is silent love and joy is spread
Around like pixie dust.

Caring for people isn't so hard it's a piece of cake
Helping for people gives you some respect
Laughing with friends is a blast.

Mates who are trustworthy are a key fact about them
So you stay out of trouble
Being quiet is good, no one will shout at you
It's being quiet as a mouse.

Ruhel Amin (12)
Hadleigh High School, Ipswich

Winter

The crisp snow glistens as it falls
Making a soft layer of sugar like snow on the frozen ground
Numbing my fingers as I make a snowman
Adding the carrot nose
On this chilly winter day
Wearing a bobble hat to keep me warm
Going inside to get warm again
Drinking hot chocolate
That I can feel trickling down my throat
On this chilly winter day.

Ella Delves (11)
Hadleigh High School, Ipswich

Narnia

Big, dark, empty room,
Now entering the wardrobe,
In a different world.

Tall trees crispy snow,
Come across Mr Tumnus,
Cold winds as we walk.

Tea, cakes and sardines,
Lovely music fall asleep,
Kidnapped by a friend.

Bells heard far away,
Edmund meets evil white witch,
Turkish delight, more!

Fall into witch trap,
Evil magic in a wand,
Now who'll win, Aslan?

Two sons of Adam
All here together at last,
Two daughters of Eve.

Katie Gant (11)
Hadleigh High School, Ipswich

Good And Evil In The Lion, The Witch And The Wardrobe

Beyond a wardrobe is a world
I never knew there was such a good
Person that could make such a place
It was like heaven but you're not dead
The queen was hell
In a land called Narnia, there is an evil
Person who should not be there
The centaurs, the dwarves and fawns are so good
Live centaurs, dwarves and fawns they have
Such fun and parties, at places called Destiny's Lawns
In the Golden Age of Narnia, reigned two kings, and queens
But from the world of Narnia, they did not come it seems.
Before the Golden Age, the white witch ruled the land,
She made it always winter all the time
And Christmas was banned forever
Any who opposed her she simply turned to stone,
And with that power in her grasp, she sat upon her throne,
So the white witch is pure, pure
Evil.

Nicole Ellis-Tattersdale (11)
Hadleigh High School, Ipswich

Magic To Reality

It's shimmery
It's like an adventure
It's enchanting with sprinkles of colourful magic
Circling your eyes
Dark, light, nice, evil reality, it's so confusing
Wondering, waiting, exploring
It's as unbelievable as crisp candyfloss
Hanging from a stick
Lick, slurp, gulp
The wonderful spoonful of magic.

Jade Richards (11)
Hadleigh High School, Ipswich

Good And Evil

Bullets are nasty
Teachers are helpful
The sun and moon are like light bulbs
Heaven is pleasing and friendly
Hell is vile and revolting
The sun is as hot as an oven and
The moon is as cool as a fridge
Gangsters are disgusting
Parents are giving.

Brett Crisp (11)
Hadleigh High School, Ipswich

Monster

A nightmare of words describe him
Hundreds of people despise him
His boomerang back doubled up
His enormous eyes open up

Portals disguised by empty cries
His wrapped muscles tense thighs
Ready . . . waiting
No reply.

Swamped dreadlocked hair
Crazy sticking up here and there
Green boggy brown cloths,
His mouth a cauldron spitting foams.

Fist clenched holding the past,
Letting nothing go, walking slow
Skin as worn as over done crust,
Undistinguished through minds of disgust.

Bone-chilling anger floods
A face of vein blood
Spread terror through the palms of his hands
Unforced hatred left in land after land.

Kate Tabrett (14)
Hadleigh High School, Ipswich

I Miss You

Under the midnight sky
You said your last goodbyes
And followed beckoning destiny

Scenes of a dream flash before my eyes
A distant but sweet memory
Like you

The sun forever shines upon you
Like being bathed in liquid love

I will always love you

I know it's no one's fault that you're gone
But it doesn't stop me wishing to the velveteen sky
Wishing that I'll see you again
Fly with you on the wings of a dream

My dreams fell apart the day you left
But they still glitter
Burning with the flame of lost ecstasy

But never forgetting what couldn't be.

Sara Rea (13)
Hadleigh High School, Ipswich

Another School Day

The bell rang for the start of the day
Registration had come and our tutor had some words to say
I had English first
By the end of the lesson I thought my head would burst
PE, drama and then DT.
There was so much dust that I could barely see
When it was lunch I was starving
It seemed ages until the bell started to ring
I had one more lesson, it was French
I couldn't wait to finish and sit on the park bench
I went to my locker to pick up my coat
When I opened it out fell a note
It read: 'see me outside', it was quarter past 3
I turned up and my music teacher stood under a tree
'Don't go yet you've got plenty more to do
You've drum lessons and I've been waiting for you'
So I didn't get home on time, what's the big deal?
I still got one of my mum's great cooked meals
Pizza and chips, the perfect recipe
The next day my English teacher said she wanted to see me
I said, 'What's the matter Miss, you wanted to see me?
Apparently I missed my tutor session at quarter past 3.

Chris Brown (13)
Hadleigh High School, Ipswich

'Bang'

Bang go the fireworks in the sky
Clap go the people in the crowd
Bang go the fireworks in the sky
Scream goes the baby in the pram
Bang go the fireworks in the sky
Howl go the dogs in the kennel
Bang go the fireworks in the sky
Zoom zoom goes the fire engine down the road
Bang go the fireworks in the sky
Cry go the people in the hospital.

Is it worth it?

Bethany-Jane Harvey (13)
Hadleigh High School, Ipswich

Seaside

Boating and bathing and digging up holes
Putting up sunshades with big wooden poles
Fishing and crabbing playing with footballs
Making sandcastles around the rock pools

Paddling, souvenirs, donkey rides, shells
Streets fumed with the fish and chip smells
Splashing around in the freezing cold sea
Huddled in beach huts with warm cups of tea

Seagulls, shrimps, seaweed and rocks
Little boats sail through the docks.

Ryan Farthing (13)
Hadleigh High School, Ipswich

Ball

My brother passes me the ball
I'm controlling it and taking a shot.
The goalie dives and scowls
As he hits the ground,
But I'm celebrating,
I've scored a goal,
Oh how I love just kicking a ball.

James Leeder (13)
Hadleigh High School, Ipswich

Things

Dogs that bark
Snakes that arc
Cats that fight
And hamsters that bite

Cars that voom
Trains that boom
Lorries that haul
And planes that fall

Everything does something.

Sam Mitchell (13)
Hadleigh High School, Ipswich

The Spirit Takes Form

A path of fire
Devoured by each stride
Stretching and reaching
A glistening hide

Arched neck laced with power
A definite line
A silhouette of beauty
Trapped in time

Muscles rippling
Sweat trickling
Time ticking
On and on

Four pools of light
Thundering on
Chasing destiny
Towards the sun

Fearless eyes
In need, in search
Gasping for breath
It scours the earth

Tail flying
Stars crying
Coat shining
On and on

A spirit so free
So wild, untamed
Flown to heaven and hell
And yet to be claimed.

Sophie Benton (14)
Hadleigh High School, Ipswich

Room

I lay in my bed listening to the tap on the window
Tap, tap, tap slowly getting louder
The shadow of a claw reached out to grab me
The flash of lightning lights up the room

My body started to freeze, my head burning up
I dare myself to get out of bed
I reach out for the curtains
My heart pounds and the tapping gets louder

I rip back the curtains
Only to find however, a woodpecker.

Sam Hunt (13)
Hadleigh High School, Ipswich

The Caterpillar

There was a caterpillar from Dover
And all he ate was clover
He went for a fly
Up high in the sky
He landed and then fell over.

Rachel Underhill (13)
Hadleigh High School, Ipswich

The Wild Mustang

Flo was the wild mare,
Who ate only pears,
She roamed the West,
And impressed the rest.

Her dark black coat
Rippled as she floated
Her emerald-green eyes
Made her look wise.

She was unable to touch,
Which annoyed the Dutch,
A beautiful beast,
Who never went East.

And that's just Flo
The wild mustang.

Shelley Horwood (13)
Hadleigh High School, Ipswich

Twinkling With Love

The sound of clattering hooves
As he elegantly canters by
Mane blowing in the wind
A shrill whinny of happiness
As he came to a halt by the gate
His warm breath filtering out
Out of his soft velvety muzzle
His eyes twinkling with love.

Jess Robeson (14)
Hadleigh High School, Ipswich

It's Always Me

These nights were sleepless with endless fights
You'll lament me constantly all through the night
Your hurtful comments keep whispering in my ears
I want to draw them out with my foot-flowing tears

Blame it on me, just blame it on me
Whilst you do though, just see your guilt free

We used to be so close, now that was a fact
But then the next road I went down had no turning back
The road brought me nothing but shouting to my ears
But at least I had nothing new to fear

Blame it all on me, just blame it on me
Whilst you do though, just set your guilt free

All through my life, I've noticed one thing
That you've never cared and you never will
It's always me every time, never you
Now why can't you see that lives so true?

Blame it all on me. Just blame it on me
And whilst you're at it, set your guilt free.

Soon you'll realise and I've brought this along
That I'm the one that's right . . . and you're the one that's wrong.

Carly Bledul (13)
Hadleigh High School, Ipswich

Good Vs Evil

Here is good. live si ereH
Bright, as bright as the stars. thgiN eht sa krad sa, kraD
Peace, goodwill, heat, optimism, guiding us through life. Gnihton gniod,
msimisseP, ssendloC, ytleurc, raW
Sun, glorious sun. wonS suoedih, wons
Laughing, smiling, leading one way. yartsa su gnidael, gninworF,
gnilkcaC
Playing. gnithgiF
Grinning over us. su revo gnicamirG
A mighty angel. nomeD ythgiM A
Tall as the mountain top. poT niatnuoM eht sa llaT

doog si ereH. Here is evil
srats eht sa thgirB sa, thgirB. Dark, as Dark as the night
efil hguorht su gnidiug, msimitpO, taeH, lliwdooG, ecaeP. War, Cruelty,
Coldness, Pessimism, doing nothing
nuS suoirolG, nuS. Snow, hideous snow
yaw eno gnidael, gnillims, gnihgual. Cackling, frowning, leading us
astray
gniyalP. Fighting
su revo gninnirG. Grimacing over us
legnA ythgiM A. A Mighty Demon
poT niatnuoM eht sa llat. Tall as the Mountain Top.

Liam Self (11)
Hadleigh High School, Ipswich

Good And Bad

Good
Helpful careful
Helping loving caring
Bad Hell Heaven kind
Rebelling disgusting damaging
Nasty horrible
Bad.

Jadene Heffer-Thorpe
Hadleigh High School, Ipswich

Good Vs Evil

Lucy is a good little girl
She is friendly and happy
She likes talking, playing and laughing
Just like her toy dolls
She thinks peace brings light to the world
But then comes the white witch
She is bad and evil just like a vampire
She likes to make people start crying
And people who like fighting and lying
She likes to make people unhappy
She thinks war and dark is good.

Sophie Green (11)
Hadleigh High School, Ipswich

Winter

It is a freezing dark night and
There is snow lining the floor
Like a crystal white carpet.

And as you walk on the snowy
Carpet it crushes and your feet
Sink into the snow and
You leave a trail of black footprints behind you.

The moon glistens in the night sky
Making the snow glisten like millions of tiny diamonds.

Max Highland (11)
Hadleigh High School, Ipswich

Dark Vs Light

Shadows creep
Lightning seeps
Darkening, frightening
You're closed in
No hope left
Until dim light glows

Thunder rumbling
Like a laughing child
And the world glows.

Madeleine Sweeting (12)
Hadleigh High School, Ipswich

Kitchen

Sit, silent, staring, soul
Happy, happy not at all
Looking at the wooden board
Fiddling with some cardboard

Wash it, chop it, colour it, serve it
Look at it, eat it, like it
Clear it, wash it, dry it, smash it

Cry, run out the way
You know you'll have to pay
Come back after a day
Look at what you did yesterday.

I didn't do it I shout and shout
I'm going to get a clout from clout
Then I shout, 'Help, help, help.'

Daniel Leathers (13)
Hadleigh High School, Ipswich

Bullseye

I'm a bullseye, a target
For my dad
Come winter, spring, I'm always sad
He comes for me through my door
Coming, coming abruptly no, no more
He says to me, 'Wake, wake get up now'
He's like a lion on a prowl
He hits me, I wake up
I stay still not knowing what's next
I'm staring right at his fake Rolex
I've got bruises everywhere
I think he's got some of my hair
I'm a bullseye, a target
For my dad.

Aidan Bignell (13)
Hadleigh High School, Ipswich

Good Vs Evil

Good
Helpful friendly
Smiling playing snowing
Good nice

Vicious devil
Bullying killing stealing
Bad bully
Evil.

Harry Evans (12)
Hadleigh High School, Ipswich

Diamond Poem

The sun is very hot
The moon is very cold
The sun is as hot as a toaster
The moon is as cold as a freezer
Youngsters are horrible
Parents are horrible
Evil is nasty
Good is kind
Hell is horrible
Heaven is nice.

Brendon Wardley (11)
Hadleigh High School, Ipswich

War Vs Peace

War
People screaming blood-curdling screams
Blood everywhere
People dying
Like there's a hunter out hunting
Evil all around
With the Devil cackling nearby
All caused by disagreements

Peace
People smiling and talking
With angels watching over them
Singing gentle songs
Laughter everywhere
Everyone getting on well together
Everything as it should be
All because people agree.

Alice Partridge (12)
Hadleigh High School, Ipswich

The Bear

The bear has a loving gentle, sensitive smile
The bear is like a little girl playing in the fields
The bear is a shaggy rug waiting to be stroked
Its claws are rough like a tree trunk;
But as smooth as a slate of marble.
Their noses are wet like a stream running through a valley
Its nose is as black as night on a winter's evening,
No light, only darkness.
The bear glares at its prey, waiting to pounce.

Georgia Dashfield (11)
Hadleigh High School, Ipswich

Peace And War

For every moment of peace
There is one of war
In the darkest times
Light can be found
In the form of a smile
In moments of sadness
Or a white dove
Above a bloodstained battlefield
Like a raging earthquake
War destroys
And like rushing rain
Peace nourishes
Peace can be a welcoming wave
War an extending fist
For every moment of peace
There is one of war.

Anastasia Wyatt (11)
Hadleigh High School, Ipswich

War And Peace

War is a black deathtrap
When the gunshot goes off the people fight
All raising their swords in rage
And fighting for freedom
Some running to help their loved ones
No one knowing if they will survive
With the winning team celebrating
Now the land is full of peace
The place where people can rest
Now the people will be happy
So now it is the land of
Peace and happiness.

Rebekah Grant (11)
Hadleigh High School, Ipswich

Diamond Poem

Living is life and loving
Life is happy and mesmerising
Living is honest trusting and celebrating

Disbelief and lies lead to war
War is shooting and killing
Bombs screaming as they fall
Innocent people dying

War leads to torturing, pain and anger
Slums dark, cold and horrid
Dying, killing and death.

Jake Howard (11)
Hadleigh High School, Ipswich

Narnia!

I walk into the wardrobe
Searching for the back, it begins
To turn cold, as I hear crunching
Footsteps as I carry on walking.

The others are coming
I can hear them talking.

I can see a shining light
It shines like a star
And is ever so bright.

I am searching for summer
Instead I see winter.

I find myself in a freaky forest
With no one around me.

There are footsteps as a creepy creature approaches me!

Mollie Hart (11)
Hadleigh High School, Ipswich

So, So, So

Evil lurking round every corner
The cold is all around
Laughing while plotting
Thinking evil things
Then evil turns to
Happiness
People thinking happy thoughts
Smiling through angel teeth
Positive with energy
Good is all around.

Rebecca Warner (11)
Hadleigh High School, Ipswich

Young Writers Information

We hope you have enjoyed reading this book - and that you will continue to enjoy it in the coming years.

If you like reading and writing poetry drop us a line, or give us a call, and we'll send you a free information pack.

Alternatively if you would like to order further copies of this book or any of our other titles, then please give us a call or log onto our website at www.youngwriters.co.uk

**Young Writers Information
Remus House
Coltsfoot Drive
Peterborough
PE2 9JX**

(01733) 890066